An ever normal granary and the solution for global economic prosperity

What we should learn from J.M.Keynes and Yamada Houkoku

Yasuhisa Miyake

UNIVERSITY EDUCATION PRESS

Contents

Preface 5
Introduction (New economics of J.M. Keynes) ... 10

Chapter 1 14
Cognition and J.M. Keynes's economic philosophy and Generative Economics
1.1 Cognitive linguistics and J.M. Keynes's economic philosophy   14
1.2 Noam Chomsky and J.M. Keynes "Empiricism and Rationalism"   16
1.3 Relevance theory and J.M. Keynes's Economic philosophy   19
1.4 Cognition and Generative Economics   22
Conclusion   24

Chapter 2 29
Homeostasis and complementary economic network
2.1 The causes of economic depression and economic disequilibrium   29
2.2 The self-adjusting mechanism and J.M. Keynes's economic solution   30

Chapter 3 .... *37*
Economic fluctuation and a cognitive phenomenon
3.1 Cognition and human inductive process   *37*
3.2 The myth of discretionary macroeconomic policy   *39*
3.3 Schema and J.M. Keynes's economic philosophy   *42*
Conclusion   *49*

Chapter 4 .... *51*
Cognition and J.M. Keynes's General theory
4.1 Logical probability and J.M. Keynes's economic philosophy

51

4.2 Rational expectation and J.M. Keynes's economic philosophy "Cognition, spontaneous deduction and Relevance"   *56*
4.3 J.M. Keynes's economic philosophy and the trade cycle   *62*

Chapter 5 .... *66*
J.M. Keynes's General theory and Yamada Houkoku's economic policy
5.1 An ever normal granary and Yamada Houkoku's economic policy   *66*
5.2 Economic network and Yamada Houkoku's solution   *79*
5.3 Complementary economic network and Yamada Houkoku's solution   *87*
5.4 The Rizairon and Yamada Houoku's economic idea   *99*

Supplements *105*
Financial crisis Great Depression and New economics for global prosperity

Part II *109*
Yamada Houkoku's solution for global economic prosperity
"The transformation from a competitive global capitalism to a complementary economic system"

Introduction *111*

1 A monetary economy and Yamada Houkoku's solution

113

2 Complex cognitive theory and Yamada Houkoku's policy

124

3 Yamada Houkoku's solution and Generative Economics "Cognition and Universal macroeconomics based upon modern linguistics" *129*

4 Yamada Houkoku's dynamic economic system   *133*

5 Yamada Houkoku's solution and a selfadjusting mechanism

141

6 Yamada Houkoku's solution for global economic prosperity

167

Conclusion *175*

References *179*

preface

This paper reveals why Yamada Houkoku's economic policy is the only solution to global economic crisis.

Taking an in-depth look at the book called "The General theory", I explain what went wrong and demonstrate why the establishment of an ever normal granary is needed to restore economic prosperity and to prevent financial crisis.

A soliton economy is the opposite of a chaos economy.

This economy implies that a small shock does not lead to economic depression and financial crisis.

A capitalist economy lacks a complementary market.

The economic system created by Yamada Houkoku maximizes the amount of exchange of goods, with a minimum detrimental effect of money on macroeconomy.

A monetary economy does not maximize the amount of exchange of goods.

A barter economy with no money also doesn't do that.

J.M. Keynes supports fiscal policy whose purpose is to increase effective demand.

On the other hand, Milton Friendman emphasizes the importance of monetary policy.

However, they don't recognize the difference between surface structure and deep structure.

A western economist except for behavioural economics seems to ignore the psychology and cognitive efficiency inherent in human beings.

Expectation plays an important role in economy.

However, modern economics ignores deep structure in expectation.

In other words, expectation is strongly related with human cognitive abilities.

Deep structure in economy belongs to human cognition the exchange of goods and economic structure etc.

Western economists seem to pay attention to only visible things.

On the other hand, Yamada Houkoku's economic policy implies that an invisible deep structure is more important than monetary or fiscal policy and a change in policy regime.

Modern macroeconomics is concerned with the notion of optimization, optimal control theory, a conflict between domestic objectives and external objectives.

On the other hand, Yamada Houkoku's economic policy is based upon the notion of Japanese or Chinese philosophy.

According to them, a conflict must be solved by the addition of new things, which creates the self-organizing emergence.

Monetary policy is intended for both the stability of exchange rates and domestic economy.

Fiscal policy is intended for both the stability of domestic economy and social welfare.

However, we can't achieve both objectives at the same time.
In a similar way, we can't say that he must can swim.
This means that we can't use auxiliary verb at the same time.
However, we can say that he must be able to swim.
He must can swim.
The above sentence is ungrammatical.
In order to correct it, we must replace can with be able to.
If we say, "He must be able to swim", that sounds natural.

The above example explains the essence of Yamada Houkoku's economic policy.

Houkoku's solution means that an ever normal granary is intended for the stability of domestic economy and social welfare.

It can contribute to an increase in fiscal revenues and the amount of exchange of goods.

In order to achieve both of the objectives of exchange rate stability and economic boom, monetary policy is not effective.

However, the establishment of an ever normal granary with monetary policy can be effective with them.

In this situation, "can" corresponds to only monetary policy, and "be able to" corresponds to an ever normal granary with monetary policy.

In a similar way, fiscal policy is not effective with both of the objective of economic boom and social welfare.

A lower interest rate may lead to economic boom.

However, it might cause exchange rate overshooting.

A higher taxes may lead to fiscal surplus, which contributes to social welfare.

However, it might lead to economic depression.

On the other hand, an ever normal granary with fiscal policy may be effective with both of them.

Linguistics literature says that can and must are not in harmony with each other in a same sentence.

However, it says that must and be able to be the exception.

In order to change an ungrammatical sentence into a grammatical one, the solution must be the replacement of a word.

Fiscal policy corresponds to "can".

On the other hand, an ever normal granary with fiscal policy corresponds to "be able to".

Globally speaking monetary and fiscal policies are not effective with respect to output exchange rate stability and equilibrium in external balance.

However "must and be able to" are different in character.

In a similar way, monetary policy and fiscal policy are the same in character if we say economically.

On the other hand, an ever normal granary with them are quite different in character.

An ever normal granary holds the function of the market design mechanism and the platform economics.

On the other hand, a great difference which distingutes Yamada Houkoku's economic model from them is as follows.

They lack the existence of complementarity and a export sector.

The business model Yamada Houkoku creates is intended for the emergence of new economic structure.

The establishment of an ever normal granary creates the economy based upon a barter economy, which buy economic goods from a private sector and sell them to people who are in need.

In other words, economic depression will come back to normal soon, without any monetary expansion.

A collapse in bubbles or stock prices leads to the emergence of people who suffer from heavy debts and a reduction of the purchasing power in money.

The solution is not expansionary monetary or fiscal policy, but the establishment of exchange of goods, which means an ever normal granary. Macroeconomic policy does not matter.

The matter is economic system, which Yamada Houkoku creates for the welfare of poor people.

Introduction (New economics of J.M. Keynes)

I would like to challenge conventional wisdom which means that discretionary macroeconomic policy is not effective with respect to output and employment.

If discretionary macroeconomic policy implies the establishment of monopoly and control system, then this policy may be effective.

J.M. Keynes's real economic message means that Government and central banks should control the amount of an exchange of goods, not interest rates and the amount of money.

The reason is that economic depression implies the reduction of the amount of an exchange of goods.

If this is true, an increase in a circulating money and its velocity corresponds with the increase in this amount.

The establishment of monopoly and control system does not lead to fiscal debts.

If this establishment leads to an increase in private firm's profit, then logic tells us that economic recovery occurs soon.

An increase in money supply does not always lead to the increase in the amount of economic transactions.

Economic recovery is conditional upon the fact that the creation of Government enterprise leads to private firm's profit.

This fact is also conditional upon the fact that the relationship between Government enterprise and private firm is complementary.

In other words, economic goods produced by Government create new demand for private firms, which leads to economic recovery.

If we try to develop J.M. Keynes's economic philosophy, we must construct economic model that the multiplier effect depends upon not only the marginal propensity to consume but also the number of complementary goods and the number of economic network.

The above argument tells us that complementary goods complements economic network each other. In other words, a great economic shock never cause a great economic depression with a great number of them.

One of the real causes of economic depression is a lack of complementary goods and economic network.

In other words, deflation (a price competition) is due to a lack of them.

If this is true, a quantitative monetary easing is not effective with respect to output and employment.

As they increase, investment uncertainty decreases, and therefore this stimulates domestic economy.

The purpose of J.M. Keynes's general theory is to tell us the mechanism of investment uncertainty.

The above argument tells us that 'new general theory' must include the solution for investment uncertainty.

Complementary goods and economic network are related with effectual demand, effective demand and division of labour, which is linked with the amount of output and employment.

The reason why comparative advantage and mutual advantage don't work in a globalized capitalist system is simply due to a lack of them.

The reason why a lack of them occurs is because of animal spirits and a strong interest for profits of a private firm.

Therefore, government and central banks must cope with this problem by producing complementary goods.

If the number of complementary goods and economic network increase, economic problems such as the redistribution of income unemployment and deflation may be solved.

If government enterprise increases the number of them, then a profit motive of them works well for a capitalist economy.

Oversupply of non-complementary goods leads to economic deflation, because of a price competition and a lack of demand.

However, if government increases the number of complementary goods, then non-complementary goods changes into complementary goods, which leads to economic recovery.

The purpose of this paper is to prove that economic philosophy of J.M. Keynes is completely misunderstood.

Economic fluctuation reflects our cognitive abilities to understand economic phenomenon.

This can't be explained by a reductionist view.

For example, the changes in financial assets, the change of a value in money, the rate of unemployment can't be controlled only by discretionary macroeconomic policy.

If J.M. Keynes were alive now, he might say that economic fluctuations can result from application of human inductive process to them.

A central theme of J.M. Keynes's economic philosophy means that economic fluctuation is purely a cognitive phenomenon.

Chapter 1

Cognition and J.M. Keynes's economic philosophy and Generative Economics

1.1 Cognitive linguistics and J.M. Keynes's economic philosophy

Economic fluctuation is not merely a phenomenon of the manipulation of monetary and fiscal policy.

In mathematical economics, economy is independent of human understanding.

In economics based upon cognition, real economic situations is to a very large extent dependent upon human mind and its conceptual system based upon imaginative aspects of reason, metaphor, schema, mental imagination.

New classical economics based upon rational expectation assumes that rational thought consists of the manipulation of abstract mathematical equations that is independent of human knowledge.

On the other hand, J.M. Keynes's approach appears to denies it.

Human mind is not the mechanical manipulation of abstract mathematical symbols.

Economy does not work like an abstract machine and a computer.

J.M. Keynes's economic philosophy is related with internal representations of external reality, imaginative capacity and human imaginative capacities.

Cognitive linguistics which emphasizes the role of schema means a mental structure which determines attention and the absorption of new knowledge.

Economic deep structure based upon an organized pattern of thought or behaviour make people pay attention to some things that fit into their schema.

This implies that they ignore exceptions and contradictions.

Economic deep structure organizes and perceives new information.

This structure helps people understand the rapidly changing economic environment.

Expectation and human economic behaviour belongs to surface structure, which is controlled by economic deep structure.

The fact that people can quickly change their behaviour is not due to rational expectation.

The reason can be explained in the following way.

If people use schema, then people don't have complex

thought.

This means that they may quickly act without any effort in a systematic change in policy regimes.

In other words, people may not change their behaviour with the systematic change, because they interpret this change and organize new perception.

1.2 Noam Chomsky and J.M. Keynes "Empiricism and Rationalism"

Human mental faculties and cognitive structure have been ignored by many economists.

Econometric analysis, empirical studies and even mathematical economic models have ignored human mind, human intelligence and human interpretation.

Human cognitive system controls people's actions and their interpretation of experience.

This implies that human cognitive structure determines economic fluctuation.

Mathematical models, econometric analysis and economic historical analysis are interested in primarily the arrangement of "facts" or "data".

Economists except J.M. Keynes did not undertake the task of studying a range of highly complex cognitive structures.

J.M. Keynes tried to construct an explanatory theory.

In other words, J.M. Keynes tried to answer the question

of how people interpret new information by using the intuitive, unconscious knowledge.

J.M. Keynes's economic philosophy criticizes scientific empiricism and explains a predetermined cognitive system.

A central theme of General Theory and probability theory is that economic fluctuation is due to an innate human cognitive capacity.

We can't explain economic fluctuation brought about human mental world by using a mechanical world.

Economic fluctuation often occurs without any economic shock and a change in policy regimes.

Each economy in each country in the world has different experience and economic data.

However, the pattern of economic fluctuation is essentially the same, probably because the human cognitive system is essentially the same.

Consequently we have to suppose that people share the same internal constraints which make economic situations and a process in the change of them quite similar.

We should abandon the methodological empirical dogma which separates human mind and cognition from economic analysis.

Empirical studies based upon mathematical model which emphasizes the collection of economic data completely ignore human mental functions.

Modern economics can be explained by skinner's behaviorism.

Rational expectation theory can be explained by stimulus-response reinforcement and operant conditioning.

However, this theory ignores "human nature".

J.M. Keynes's economic philosophy implies much criticism of induction approaches and this emphasizes human knowledge and the interpretation of economic facts based upon it.

In other words, his philosophy means the economics of inference and cognition.

The inference based upon human cognition is quite different from the deductions of mathematical logic in the sense that the conclusions are only probable.

Noam Chomsky says in the following way.

> Generative grammar is form of the break with and in opposition to structuralism.
>
> The latter, in general, is conceived of linguistics as a classificatory activity.
>
> You have given the discipline a logical structure a scientific structure.
>
> The term science is perhaps honorific. My own inclination is to attach less importance to the precise description of some domain of linguistic data than to the explanatory power and depth of underlying principles[1].

Mathematical equation does not imply "a creative aspect of human beings" human psychology human mind and human cognition.

Econometric analysis or empirical studies based upon mathematical equation just simply means the precise description of economic data.

In other words, this approach does not imply the explanation of deep and underlying principles which determine and control economic data, economic reality and economic situations.

Only J.M. Keynes's economic philosophy gives us explicit human principles for determining economic structures.

Current economic theories do not undertake the task of studying a range of highly complex economic structures, although Adam Smith and Karl Marx did it and tried to clarity the role of human nature in economics[2].

1.3 Relevance theory and J.M. Keynes's Economic philosophy

Economic deep structure is based upon the universal cognitive tendency to maximize relevance.

This implies that monetary and fiscal policy alone does not make it possible to predict and manipulate the mental states of people.

In other words, the effectiveness of macroeconomic

policy depends upon the activation of an appropriate set of contextual assumptions.

The above argument tells us that a Lucas critique and rational expectation is related with a positive cognitive effect and context.

Deirdre Wilson and Dan Sperber says in the following way.

> The most important type of cognitive effect is a contextual implication, a conclusion deducible from input and context together, but from neither input nor context alone.
>
> For example, on seeing my train arriving I might look at my watch, access my knowledge of the train timetable, and derive the contextual implication that my train is late which may itself achieve relevance by combining with further contextual assumptions to yield further implications.
>
> Other types of cognitive effect include the strengthening, revision, or abandonment of available assumptions.
>
> For example, the sight of my train arriving late might confirm my impression that the service is deteriorating, or make me alter my planes to do some shopping on the way to work.
>
> According to relevance theory, an input is relevant to an individual when, and only when, its processing yields such positive cognitive effects.
>
> According to relevance theory, other things being equal,

the greater the positive cognitive effects achieved by processing an input, the greater its relevance will be.

Thus, the sight of my train arriving one minute late may make little worthwhile difference to my representation of the world, while the sight of it arriving half an hour late may lead to a radical reorganization of my day, and the relevance of the two inputs will vary accordingly[3].

J.M. Keynes's economic philosophy is related with human mind and can be explained in the following way.

The universal cognitive tendency to maximize relevance makes it possible to control the mental states of others, which lead to economic stability and the prevention of financial crisis.

Therefore it implies an inferential economics.

Logic tells us that macroeconomic theory is a cognitive psychological theory.

A central theme of his economic philosophy and General Theory is that relevance is a basic feature of human cognition.

If this is true, the effectiveness of macroeconomic policy depends upon the fact that it is relevant to people when it connects with background information they have.

In other words, macroeconomic policy is effective, if it is relevant to them when its processing in a context of available assumptions yields a positive cognitive effect.

This means that this policy is effective if its effect is a worthwhile difference to their representation of the real economic situations[4].

1.4 Cognition and Generative Economics

A change in deep structure for the recovery from economic depression is related with the number of complementary goods between each sector in the whole economy.

Evolutionary deep structure implies a change in the complementary relationship between public sector's goods and private sector's goods.

An ever normal granary contributed to adaptive deep structure, which adjusts the mismatch between demand and supply, and makes unsold commodities into the power of exchange.

Economic depression is due to the fact that supply doesn't create its own demand.

A change in deep structure creates a change in surface structure.

Surface structure implies economic depression, unemployment and unstable prices.

We can't control and stabilize a change in surface structure by monetary or fiscal policy and a change in policy regimes (a change in expectation).

The reason is as follows.

Deep structure controls surface structure.

Discretionary macroeconomic policy can't control deep structure.

A change in this structure is conditional upon the fact that public sector creates complementary goods which increases the demand for a private sector's goods.

Charles Goodhart law can be explained in the following way.

When economic policy is used for control purposes, it ceases to be a predictable variable.

If Government attempts to control any economic variable then, they become unreliable.because a private sector anticipate the effect and change her behaviour.

Lucas critique implies that it is impossible to forecast the effect of a change in economic policy on the basis of an observed historical data[5].

Charles Goodhart law and Lucas critique are in conformity with J.M. Keynes's economic philosophy.

Because of the paradox of poverty, macroeconmic policy is not effective. If J.M. Keynes were alive in a wealthy community, he would argue that a change in deep structure is the solution for economic recovery.

The doctrine itself has remained unquestioned by orthodox economists, up to the latest date, that J.M. Keynes's economic philosophy is Government intervention (discretionary monetary and fiscal policy).

In a similar way, they never challenged conventional wisdom that a multiplier effect depends upon the marginal propensity to consume.

However, what J.M. Keynes ignored is the fact that the number and extent of interaction in economic network and web determine its effect.

A change in deep structure leads to the fact that the classical theory represents the way in which we should like our economy to behave and it actually does.

J.M. Keynes's solution means the establishment of international stabilization fund, which provides for full employment and equitable distribution of wealth and incomes.

Discretionary macroeconomic policy doesn't contribute to the solution because of its failure to provide for them.

Any mathematical model based upon J.M. Keynes's economic philosophy, ignores human psychology human mind and human cognition.

This means that any economic model does not imply "a creative aspect" of human beings.

Conclusion

General Theory is intended to prove that one of the causes of economic fluctuation is due to the fact that a degree of belief could be rational.

The reason is as follows.

J.M. Keynes's human conception can be explained by "relevance".

A degree of belief always fluctuates, depending upon old evidence and new evidence.

In other words, an interaction between old information and new information changes the degree of belief.

Rational expectation implies the fact that a degree of belief could be rational.

J.M. Keynes tried to explain it in terms of a frequency theory and was unsuccessful in defining the meaning of probability.

However, J.M. Keynes made a great mistake in the sense that it is not logical.

The reason is as follows.

The relevant evidence increases subjective probability.

If new evidence is relevant, the weight is not left unchanged.

Probability is always subjective and unstationary because context background knowledge and schema include old information and new information.

Relevance is related with cognitive efficiency.

Economic fluctuation and instability inherent within a capitalist system are due to the fact that they are interrelated each other.

Probability is not logical and can't be estimated by mathematical equation.

Economy change because of human misunderstanding of the real economic situations.

Thus, there is room for us to intervene in the market.

Note
(1) Noam Chomsky
   On Language
   Chomsky's classic works
   Language and in one volume
   Responsibility and reflections on language
   The New Press 1998 p106
(2) Noam Chomsky says in the following way.
   Any serious social science or theory of social change must be founded on some concept of human nature.

   A theorist of classical liberalism such as Adam Smith beings by affirming that human nature is defined by a propensity to track and barter to exchange goods: that assumption accords very well with the social order he defends.

   If you accept that premise (which is hardly credible), it turns out that human nature conforms to an idealized early capitalist society, without monopoly, without state intervention, and without social control of production.

   If on the contrary, you believe with Marx or the French and German Romantics that only social cooperation permits the full development of human powers, you will then have a very different picture of a desirable society.

   There is always some conception of human nature, implicit or explicit, underlying a doctrine of social order or social change.

   Noam Chomsky
   On Language
   Chomsky's classical works

Language and in one volume Responsibility and reflections on language
The New Press P70, 71
(3) Deirdre Wilson and Dan Sperber Chapter 27
Relevance theory
The handbook of pragmatics edited by Laurence R, Horn and Gregory Ward
Blackwell Publishing 2004 P608-610
(4) J.M. Keynes's economic philosophy can be understood from the perspective of relevance theory

J.M. Keynes says in the following way.

Relevance is an important term in probability of which the meaning is readily intelligence.

In the first we consider whether or not x is to be preferred to y on evidence h_1 in the second we consider whether the addition of h_1 to evidence h is relevant to x.

It will be convenient to define also two other phrases if h_1 and h_2 are independent and complementary parts of the evidence between them they make up h and neither can be inferred from the other.

If x is the conclusion and h_1 and h_2 are independent and complementary parts of the evidence, then h_1 is relevant if the addition of it to h_2 affects the probability of x.

The collected writings of John Maynard Keynes volume VIII
A treatise on probability Macmillan 1973 P58, 59 P113
(5) Thought is embodied, that is the structures used to put together our conceptual systems grow out of bodily experience and make sense in terms of it, moreover, the core of our conceptual systems is directly grounded in perception, body movement, and experience of a physical and social character.

Thought is imaginative, in that those concept which are not directly grounded in experience employ metaphor, metonymy, and mental imagery—all of which go beyond the literal mirroring or representation of external reality.

It is this imaginative capacity that allows for "abstract" thought and takes the mind beyond what we can see and feel.

The imaginative capacity is also embodied –indirectly– since the metaphors metonymies and images are based on experience, often bodily experience.

George Lakoff Women, Fire and Dangerous things What Categories reveal about the mind, the University of Chicago Press 1987.

Chapter 2

Homeostasis and complementary economic network

2.1 The causes of economic depression and economic disequilibrium

One of the causes of economic depression and economic disequilibrium is partly due to the fact that consumption and investment do not increase at a proportional rate[1].

Therefore, economic solution is not an increase in consumption and investment but an increase in the number of exchange of goods and complementary economic network.

They contribute to a proportional rate of increase in consumption and investment.

In other words, the obvious government intervention is not monetary and fiscal policy but a creation of complementary economic network.

Economic deflation dominates a global capitalist economy because of an excess supply of goods and a lack of innovation and economic diversity.

Expansionary monetary and fiscal policy does not create innovation, economic diversity and complementary economic network.

2.2 The self-adjusting mechanism and J.M. Keynes's economic solution

The self-adjusting mechanism in a market economy does not always work because of the characteristics of money.

In other words, the injection of Homeostasis into the market economy implies the establishment of an ever normal granary which creates complementary economic network [2].

If every country produces the same kinds of economic goods, this leads to economic deflation.

The economic solution is not an increase in monetary expenditures but an increase in the number of exchange of goods.

One of the causes of "a poverty of richness" is a nonlinear relationship between consumption and income.

This means that a diminishing decrease in demand for new investment occurs because people become rich.

Economic disequilibrium in the rich countries is partly due to a poverty of richness, according to J.M. Keynes.

The obvious solution is an increase in the number of exchange of goods and the creation of complementary economic network,

Chapter 2 Homeostasis and complementary economic network 31

which are supposed to lead to the increase in the injection of money in every branch of domestic economy.

Economic depression is due to the fact that every country produces an excess amount of the same kinds of economic goods[3].

An ever normal granary and the Buffer stock scheme imply automatic adjustment mechanism which increases the number of exchange of goods.

J.M. Keynes's solution does not necessarily mean any government intervention, discretionary macroeconomic policy and fiscal expenditures based upon fiscal debts.

Prices fixed, cartel arrangements and amalgamations implies automatic adjustment mechanism which prevents a weak selling[4].

Thus his economic philosophy means the establishment of market economy based upon automatic adjustment mechanism which increases employment effective demand and income (consumption).

Unemployment is primarily due to an unwillingness of capitalists to employ employee at a higher wage.

Therefore Government must create new government-financed firms to employ employee at a higher wage.

Employment depends upon not only effective demand but also the number of economic network and an increase in exchange of goods.

A solution of the unemployment problem could not be

achieved by monetary and fiscal policy.

That weapon is not powerful enough by itself to overcome this problem because the amount of employment depends upon the willingness of capitalist to employ employee.

Thus, Government must create new firms which are willing to employ employee at a higher wage.

J.M. Keynes's economic solution means the establishment of economic system that does not need any government intervention.

His solution implies automatic adjustment mechanism which is like a Homeostasis system in a living system.

The reason is because his philosophy is influenced by a classical Chinese philosophy and economic history, medicine and the philosophy of language, and therebore J.M. Keynes's economic philosophy is misunderstood[5].

His economic solution is based upon the following argument.

Creditor nations and deficit nations are mutually interdependent each other.

Therefore we must transform from economic model based upon perfect competition to the model based upon a win-win relationship between them[6].

Note
(1) J.M. Keynes says in the following way.
    It is also obvious from the above that the employment of a given number of men on public works will (on the assumptions made) have a much larger effect on aggregate employment at a time when there is

Chapter 2   Homeostasis and complementary economic network   33

severe unemployment, than it will have later on when full employment is approached.

In the above example, if at a time when employment has fallen to 5,200,000, an additional 100,000 men are employed on public works, total employment will rise to 6,400,000.

But if employment is already 9,000,000 when the additional 100,000 men are taken on for public works, total employment will only rise to 9,200,000.

Thus public works even if doubtful utility may pay for themselves over and over again at a time of severe unemployment if only from the diminished cost of relief expenditure provided that we can assume that a smaller proportion of income is saved when unemployment is greater, but they may become a more doubtful proportion as a state of full employment is approached.

Furthermore, if our assumption is correct that the marginal propensity to consume falls off steadily as we approach full employment, it follows that it will become more and more troublesome to secure a further given increase of employment by further increasing investment.

John Maynard Keynes
The general theory of employment interest and money
Macmillan 1949 P127
(2) Walter Bradford Cannon
Wisdom of the Body
Kegon Paul, Trubner and Company 1932
(3) R.F. Harrod says in the following way.

He advised some kind of compulsory cartel to be enforced by the Federation and the Banks.

This should adopt a system of transferable quotas, so that production might be concentrated in the most efficient mills.

Then there was the project of quotas of output for each distinct section of the trade.

The association was to have a small capital and Keynes saw therein the possibility of working out a scheme of co-operative credit by which fresh working capital might be found.

He thought the association would provide a framework within which more fully developed cartel arrangements and amalgamations could be gradually organized, and adjured the banks to support it.

R.F. Harrod
The Life of John Maynard Keynes
Macmillan 1952 P380-382

(4) An automatic adjustment mechanism can be explained by the following J.M. Keynes's argument.

The IMCU system must have a built-in mechanism that encourages any nation that runs persistent trade surpluses of exports over imports to spend what is deemed (in advance) by agreement of the international community to be "excessive" credit balances (savings) of foreign liquid reserve assets that have been deposited in the nation's deposit account at the IMCU.

These accumulated credits (savings out of international earned income) represent funds that the creditor nation could have used to buy the products of foreign industries but instead used to increase its foreign reserves in terms of its deposit at the IMCU.

This involves the recognition that when a nation holds excessive credits in its deposit account at the IMCU, these excess credits are creating unemployment problems and the lack of profitable opportunities for enterprises somewhere in the global economy.

Paul Davidson
The Keynes solution
The path to Global economic prosperity 2009 P137-141

(5) R.F. Harrod says in the following way.

Since there was a marked reluctance to adopt his own definitions of income and saving, which made sense of his treatise theory, he thought that the only way to extricate himself from the tangle was to revert to the plain, straightforward book-keeping usage, by which saving and investment must necessarily be equal.

Chapter 2 Homeostasis and complementary economic network 35

Consequently, he could no longer say that in any circumstances saving would be unequal to investment.

What happened then if producers, blindly disregarding the fact that at full employment saving would be greater than desired investment chose to produce so much as to give full employment?

Saving would in fact still be equal to investment.

But the excessive propensity to save in relation to investment opportunities would compel producers either to accumulate unwanted stocks or sell at prices which they deemed inadequate.

The unwanted stocks would constitute investment, if prices were so low as to entail losses, these would have to be deducted from the savings of the community at large and on this basis investment would be equal to saving.

But the position would clearly be one of disequilibrium it was the kind of position investigated in the Treatise, accumulating stocks and inadequate prices would lead to a reduction of orders and growing unemployment, and this process would continue until stocks ceased to accumulate and marginal production received an adequate remuneration.

R.F. Harrod
The life of John Maynard Keynes
Macmillan 1952 P456

The above argument tells us that J.M. Keynes's economic philosophy must be influenced by a classical Chinese economic system (monetary and control system).

(6) Paul Davidson says in the following way.

If the creditor nation spends its excess credits, this spending will increase profit opportunities and the hiring of workers around the globe and thereby promote global full employment.

Spending excessive credits to create profits and jobs in other nations.

This means more income for people and businesses in the nations experiencing unfavorable balances of trade and who were following from foreigners to buy their excess imports over exports.

In essence, spending in this way give deficit nations the opportunity to work their way out of international debt by earning additional income by selling additional exports to their creditors.

Paul Davidson
The Keynes solution
The path to global economic prosperity Macmillan 2009 P138

Chapter 3
Economic fluctuation and a cognitive phenomenon

3.1 Cognition and human inductive process

Economic fluctuations may emerge upon presentation of economic data, a change in policy regimes, announcement and discretionary macroeconomic policy.

If J.M. Keynes were alive now, he might say that economic fluctuations can result from application of human inductive process to them.

A central theme of J.M. Keynes's economic philosophy means that economic fluctuation is purely a cognitive phenomenon.

J.M. Keynes's economic philosophy means that economics is part of psychology that pays attention to human cognition and mind.

The hypothesis of rational expectations clarify the fact that patterns will vary systematically with changes in government policies. Macroeconomics took a new turn and did undergo remarkable developments because of rational expectation revolution but this theory owed nothing to cognition.

In other words, this theory may belong to a skinner's reinforcement theory and can't explain human mind behind human reaction.

A human reaction based upon a change in policy regimes involves an interaction between discretionary macroeconomic policy and people's background knowledge.

This hypothesis just abstracts out the human response to a change in policy regimes and new information.

How people set about narrowing down and choosing among many possibilities depends upon an inferential process.

Many economists have not described economic fluctuations as this process.

In other words, human mental process has not been described.

An immediate human reaction based upon a change in policy regimes could be explained by the following fact.

People could understand the mental state of policy makers and expectation played an important role in interpretation.

In other words, the immediate human reaction can't happen unless the intention of policy makers is interpreted in a particular way.

Logical probability implies the degree of confirmation of the hypothesis h by the evidence e.

This implies that an immediate human reaction means the confirmation and a change in policy regimes means the

Chapter 3 Economic fluctuation and a cognitive phenomenon

evidence.

A human reaction implies the choice that people chose among many possibilities as the result of narrowing down them.

A mismatch between the context created by policy makers and the one supplied by people may result in the fact that any economic fluctuation never occur or discretionary macroeconomic policy is not effective.

Economic bubble may occur when people look at the same context or situations and do not identify them differently.

In other words, they may not impose different interpretations on new information and therefore economic fluctuations are due to the fact that people recognized economic facts and shared mutual knowledge.

3.2 The myth of discretionary macroeconomic policy

Although the Lucas critique singled out the importance of human mind, this theory must be criticized by Noam Chomsky[1].

The mathematical model of expectation must be constructed by an interaction between old information and new information.

Economic fluctuations and the effectiveness of discretionary macroeconomic policy depend upon cognitive efficiency.

A change in policy regimes produces a certain response of

people in a certain situation.

According to recent macroeconomic models, the objectives of macroeconomic policies can be achieved by a change in policy regimes with people who have rational expectation.

On the other hand, according to the deep structure model, they are achieved by the fact that policy makers provide evidence of their intentions and people inferring their intentions from the evidence.

The effectiveness of discretionary macroeconomic policy may differ because of their different interpretation on them.

In other words, our cognitive abilities control economic fluctuations[2].

Note

(1) For example, there is interesting recent work suggesting that we have images that share fundamental properties with pictorial representation.

These are mental images in the sense of this discussion, how they are physically represented is unknown and irrelevant in the present context.

Hilary Putnam, who firmly rejects the museum myth, accepts as plausible the conclusion that the brain stores images and also insists that on any plausible theory the brain does something like computation from which it follows that a theory of mind should include some notion of mental representation and rule.

Noam Chomsky
Rules and Representations
Basil Blackwell 1982 P14

Humboldt concludes that one cannot really teach language but can

Chapter 3 Economic fluctuation and a cognitive phenomenon 41

only present the conditions under which it will develop spontaneously in the mind in its own way.

Thus the form of a language, the schema for its grammar, is to a large extent given, though it will not be available for use without appropriate experience to set the language-forming processes into operation.

Like Leibniz, he reiterates the Platonistic view that, for the individual, learning is largely a matter of wiedererzeugung, that is of drawing out what is innate in the mind.

This view contrasts sharply with the empiricist notion (the prevailing modern view) that language is essentially an adventitious construct, taught by "conditioning" (as would be maintained, for example, by Skinner or Quine) or by drill and explicit explanation (as was claimed by Wittgenstein) or built up by elementary "data-processing" procedures (as modern linguistics typically maintains), but in any event, relatively independent in its structure of any innate mental faculties.

In short, empiricist speculation has characteristically assumed that only the procedures and mechanisms for the acquisition of knowledge constitute an innate property of the mind.

Thus for Hume, the method of "experimental reasoning" is a basic instinct in animals and humans, on a par with the instinct which teaches a bird, with such exactness, the art of incubation, and the whole economy and order of its nursery-it is derived from the original hand of nature.

On the other hand, rationalist speculation has assumed that the general form of a system of knowledge is fixed in advance as a disposition of the mind and the function of experience is to cause this general schematic structure to be realized and more fully differentiated.

Noam Chomsky
Aspects of the theory of syntax
The MIT Press 1965 P51-52

(2) Ronald W. Langacker says in the following way.

Think of them as graphs of stock market values, partial shape specifications, or whatever they are the same.

Our cognitive ability to conceptualize situations at varying levels of schematicity is undeniable.

As recurrent events become entrenched to form established routices, the nature of this experience becomes more and more elaborately structured.

At any given moment a brain is the locus of countless ongoing events of great complexity and diversity, but typically they are sufficiently patterned and integrated that many facets of this welter of activity constitute a coherent body of interpreted experience rather than a flux of unfamiliar and unrelated sensations.

Fundamental to cognitive processing and the structuring of experience is our ability to compare events and register any contrast or discrepany between them.

Ronald W. Langacker
Foundations of Cognitive Grammar volume I
Theoretical Prerequisites
Stanford University Press 1987 P99-101

3.3 Schema and J.M. Keynes's economic philosophy

We have schema of economic policy and economic activities.

Our schema influences the way we perceive economic policy and make decisions on economic activities.

For example, expansionary fiscal policy may activate schematic images that lead some firms to increase new investment and employment.

On the other hand, expansionary fiscal policy may activate schematic images that lead other firms to decrease investment

Chapter 3 Economic fluctuation and a cognitive phenomenon

and employment.

Our schema enhances our perception of economic policy and then our mental images are activated so that we pay attention to only information that is consistent with the image.

Expansionary fiscal policy is effective if it activates schematic images that lead all firms to increase investment and employment.

All economic fluctuations are purely due to the fact that we pay attention to information that is consistent with our mental images.

The effectiveness of a change in policy regimes depends upon the degree of economic policy that is consistent with our mental images.

As the gap between economic policy and our mental images become smaller, this effectiveness increases.

In other words, as the gap between economic policy and our mental images become larger, this effectiveness tends to decrease.

New classical economics with rational expectation hypothesis ignore the fact that directing attention to a particular focus in a given context changes economic circumstances.

The degree of effectiveness of discretionary macroeconomic policy depends upon attention and focuses in a given context not the degree of anticipation or expectation.

If this is true, people are directing attention to a particular focus such as fiscal deficit taxes inflation and unemployment.

If schematic notion common to a lower interest rate an increase in money supply and fiscal deficit is individually symbolized by inflation expansionary monetary and fiscal policy leads to inflation.

However, schematic notion common to them is not constant because of the gap between actual economic results and people's assumption.

The gap between them modifies their schematic notion.

If schematic notion common to them is individually symbolized by output and employment, they are effective with respect to output and employment.

Schematic notion corresponds to the amount of people's background knowledge.

This always changes because additional knowledge or evidence increases the certainty in judgment (the degree of rational justification).

A change in policy regimes implies additional knowledge (evidence).

The effectiveness of a change in policy regimes is determined by people's encyclopedic memory and mental activity.

They interpreted the change in them by combining new information (a change in policy regimes) with their background assumptions.

People's induction and inference determine the effectiveness of discretionary macroeconomic policy.

Chapter 3 Economic fluctuation and a cognitive phenomenon

A change in policy regimes leads to a modification of people's cognitive environment, provided that their cognitive resources are optimally allocated to maximize relevance.

The point is that a change in policy regimes or discretionary macroeconomic policy must be relevant enough to be worth people's attention.

Economic policy makers must attract people's attention and they must focus it on their intentions.

We need to examine the paradigm called the ineffectiveness of discretionary macroeconomic policy critically.

Rationality means the degree of relevance.

Irrationality means the degree of relevance.

Economic bubble and the collapse in economic bubble could be measured in terms of the degree of relevance.

Rational expectation hypothesis ignores the fact that the effectiveness of discretionary macroeconomic policy depends upon the state of knowledge of people when Government changes a policy regime.

In other words, this effectiveness depends upon the relationship between a change in policy regimes and people's interpretations.

Rational expectation hypothesis must be a psychological model for understanding the cognitive interpretation of a change in policy regimes as well as an inferential model.

This means that a change in policy regimes is just one of many inputs that can affect interpretation.

Relevance theory tells us that the thing that causes an input to stand out from others is its relevance to people or a change in policy regime.

Rational expectation ignores the fact that the message or a change in policy regimes must draw attention.

Relevance theory tells us that the thing that makes people pay attention to a change in policy regimes is its relevance to people.

Different interpretations about the future movement of economy occur to people's mind if a change in policy regimes happens.

The interpretation a rational person chooses depends upon the set of available contextual assumptions.

The central theme of rational expectation is people's perception their expectations their selfish behaviours and the relevant or interrelated measures.

Thomas J. Sargent says in the following way.

> The essential measures that ended hyperinflation in Germany, Austria, Hungary and Poland were first, the creation of an independent central bank that was legally committed to refuse the government's demand for additional unsecured credit and, second, a simultaneous alternation in the fiscal policy regime.
> <u>These measures were interrelated and coordinated.</u>
> The change that ended the hyperinflations was not

isolated restrictive actions within a given set of rules of the game or general policy[1].

If this is true, some unpleasant rational expectation hypothesis holds.

When there is a change in the government strategy or regime private economic agents do not always change their behaviours.

The reason is that this economics is based upon an instantaneous induction based upon rational beliefs, which depends upon an inadequate knowledge.

Rational expectation means a spontaneous deduction.

Spontaneous deduction creates miscalculation, which leads to new investment.

This deduction ignores other interpretations.

The uncertain human mind creates overinvestment.

Uncertainty in J.M. Keynes's mind means that supply is not always equal to demand.

A change in policy regimes in the context of existing assumptions must improve people's knowledge by adding a new piece of information, which leads to their revision of their existing assumptions.

When economic depression occurs, the amount of exchange of goods decreases, which leads to the further decrease in economic transaction.

On the other hand, when economic boom occurs, the amount of exchange of goods increases, which leads to the further increase in economic transactions.

This leads to miscalculation and misinvestment.

In other words, economic boom includes economic depression.

Economic philosophy of J.M. Keynes can be summarized as follows.

Expansionary monetary or fiscal policy does not contribute to the increase in the amount of exchange of goods or economic transactions.

J.M. Keynes's economic solution means Government's deliberate policy for an increase in economic transactions.

J.M. Keynes's economic philosophy means that a falling off in effective demand is not controlled by expansionary monetary and fiscal policy.

This also tells us that excess demand through the stimulus of inflated prices is not controlled by a higher interest rate.

The trade cycle can't be controlled by project of public works and expansionary monetary or fiscal policy.

J.M. Keynes believes that economic boom is destined to lead to economic depression. Say's law says that supply creates demand J.M. Keynes's philosophy says that this is wrong.

However, demand does not necessarily create supply.

On the other hand, the supply of complementary goods creates new demand for other economic goods.

This means that Government should create the number of complementary goods in order to increase economic

Chapter 3 Economic fluctuation and a cognitive phenomenon 49

diversity and then the self-adjusting mechanism in the market works smoothly.

In other words, economic diversity creates new economic diversity.

If Government purchase economic goods from a private sector create complementary goods and sell them to him, then we can take both.

This means that fiscal debts and deflation never occur.

Conclusion

Any mathematical model or econometric evidence can't explain the reason why economic fluctuations occurred.

Hyperinflation implies the mental process that people prefer economic goods to money.

Deflation implies the mental process that people prefer money to economic goods.

Hyperinflation and Deflation belong to surface structure.

On the other hand, these processes belong to deep structure.

The above argument tells us that the control of people's cognitive abilities leads to the stability of economic fluctuations.

Deep structure creates economic fluctuations, surface structure such as economic data conceals a fundamental level of human consciousness.

Discretionary macroeconomic policy alone can't influence economic fluctuations.

If economic fluctuation is a cognitive phenomenon, then economic solution must be analyzed in terms of human mind and consciousness.

Note
(1) Thomas J. Sargent
    Rational expectations and inflation
    Hyper Collins College Division 1986 P97-101

Chapter 4
Cognition and J.M. Keynes's General theory

4.1 Logical probability and J.M. Keynes's economic philosophy

Most work in macroeconomic theory so far has focused on mathematical models rather than the interpretation of a change in policy regimes.

J.M. Keynes's economic philosophy implies that the effectiveness of macroeconomic policy depends upon people's interpretation.

He tried to analyze positive and negative cognitive effects.

If we analyze the relationship between logical probability and J.M. Keynes's economic philosophy, the following conclusion can be derived.

The degree of confirmation depends upon the relevance between each variable[1].

J.M. Keynes's economic philosophy can be explained as follows.

The success of government intervention is conditional upon the fact that economic policy makers understand people's attention.

Attention automatically tends to go to what is most relevant at the time and therefore the effectiveness of macroeconomic policy depends upon the people taking the policy to be relevant enough to be worthy of attention.

They must indicate, by making new policy, that they regard the policy as relevant[2].

The human tendency to maximize relevance makes it possible for policy makers to predict, control and influence people's behaviours[3].

In other words, the general theory must be intended to analyze and clarity positive and negative cognitive effects.

J.M. Keynes must aim at explaining how policy makers can influence their thoughts, which leads to a change in their behaviours[4].

J.M. Keynes's treatise on probability proves that the effectiveness of macroeconomic policy depends upon the degree of confirmation[5].

Note
(1) Many empiricist authors have rejected the logical concept of probability, as distinguished from probability, because they believe that its use violates the principle of empiricism and that, therefore, probability is the only concept admissible for empiricism and hence for science.
One of the reasons given for this view is as follows.

Chapter 4 Cognition and J.M. Keynes's General theory

The concept of probability is applied also in cases in which the hypothesis h is a prediction concerning a particular event, e.g. the prediction that it will rain tomorrow or that the next throw of this die will yield an ace.

Some philosophers believe that an application of this kind violates the principle of verifiability (or confirmability).

They might say, for example, how can the statement the probability of rain tomorrow on the evidence of the given meteorological observation is one-fifth be verified?

We shall observe either rain or not rain tomorrow, but we shall not observe anything that can verify the value one-fifth.

This objection, however, is based on a misconception concerning the nature of the probability statement.

This statement does not ascribe the probability value one-fifth to tomorrow's rain but rather to a certain logical relation between the prediction of rain and the meteorological report.

Since the relation is logical, the statement is if true, L-true, therefore it is not in need of verification by observation of tomorrow's weather or of any other facts.

The situation may be clarified by a comparison with deductive logic.

Let h be the sentence there will be rain tomorrow and j the sentence there will be rain and wind tomorrow.

Suppose somebody makes the statement in deductive logic h follows logically from j.

Generally speaking, the assertion of purely logical sentences, whether in deductive or in inductive logic, can never violate empiricism if they are false, they violate the rules of logic.

The principle of empiricism can be violated only by the assertion of a factual sentence without a sufficient empirical foundation or by the thesis of apriorism when it contends that for knowledge with respect to certain factual sentences no empirical foundation is required.

The fact that probability is relative to given evidence and that therefore a complete statement of probability must contain a reference to the evidence is very important.

Keynes was the first to emphasize this relativity.

Rudolf Carnap
Logical Foundations of Probability
The University of Chicago Press 1950 P30, 31

(2) Relevance, as characterized in relevance theory is a property of inputs include external stimuli (e.g. utterances) and internal representations (e.g. memories or conclusions of inferences, which may then be used as premises for further inferences).

When is an input relevant?

An input is relevant to an individual when processing it in a context of previously available assumptions yields positive cognitive effects: that is improvements to the individual's knowledge that could not be achieved by processing either the context on its own or the new input on its own.

These improvements may consist in the derivation of contextual implications, the correction of errors and also, arguably, the reorganization of knowledge so as to make it more appropriate for future use.

Inputs are not just relevant or irrelevant, when relevant, they are more or less so.

What makes some inputs worth processing is a relatively high degree of relevance.

Many of the potential inputs competing for an individual's processing resources at a given time may offer a modicum of relevance, but few are likely to be relevant enough to deserve attention.

What makes these inputs worth processing is, in the first place, that they yield comparatively greater cognitive effects.

However, two inputs that yield the same amount of cognitive effect may differ in the amount of processing effort required to produce this effect.

Obviously, the less the effort, the better.

If relevance is what makes an input worth processing then the relevance of an input is not just a matter of the cognitive effect it yields, but also of the mental effort it requires.

Chapter 4 Cognition and J.M. Keynes's General theory

Deirdre Wilson and Dan Sperber
Meaning and Relevance
Cambridge University Press 2012 P279, 282

(3) Relevance theory claims that because of the way our cognitive system has evolved, humans have an automatic tendency to maximize relevance, as a result of constant selection pressure to words increasing efficiency, our perceptual mechanisms tend automatically to pick out potentially relevant stimuli, our memory mechanisms tend automatically to store and when appropriate, retrieve potentially relevant pieces of knowledge, and our inferential mechanisms tend spontaneously to process these inputs in the most productive way.

This spontaneous tendency to maximize relevance makes it possible to predict to some extent which available stimuli people will pay attention to and how they will process them.

Deirdre Wilson and Dan Sperber
Meaning and Relevance
Cambridge University Press 2012 P279, 282

(4) Suppose the new evidence i is added to the prior evidence e for a hypothesis.

If the posterior confirmation c (h, e, i) is higher than the prior confirmation c (h, e), i is said to be positive to h on the evidence e.
If it is lower, i is said to be negative.
In both cases i is called relevant.

The chief question to be investigated is how the c of h is influenced by the addition of i to e.
These concepts are due to Keynes.

Rudolf Carnap
Logical Foundation of Probability
The University of Chicago Press 1950 P341. 368

(5) There are two principal explicanda, two fundamentally different meanings of the word 'probability' in presystematic use.

(i) Probability 1 = degree of confirmation and (ii) probability 2 =

relative frequency.

The following is a simple and plausible classification of probability into three groups.

(i) The classical conception originated by Jacob Bernoulli systematically developed by Laplace and represented by their followers in various forms; here, probability is defined as the ratio of the number of favorable cases to the number of all possible cases.

(ii) The conception of probability as a certain objective logical relation between propositions (or sentences), the chief representatives of this concept are John maynard, Keynes and Harold Jeffrey.

(iii) The conception of probability as relative frequency.

Rudolf Carnap
Logical Foundation of probability
The University of Chicago Press 1950 P23, 24

4.2 Rational expectation and J.M. Keynes's economic philosophy "Cognition, spontaneous deduction and Relevance"

A systematic change in human behaviour may occur with a change in policy regimes, or discretionary macroeconomic policy.

Its probability depends upon people's spontaneous deduction, which implies the interaction between old information and new information.

The validity of its probability increases as the degree of relevance between old information and new information.

The probability that a systematic change in human behaviour

occurs increases as the degree of relevance between old information and new information increases.

The cognitive efficiency brings about spontaneous deduction which leads to rational expectation, which is human mind with the highest degree of relevance between old information and new information.

It causes a high correlation between one variable and another variable.

On the other hand, the lowest degree of relevance leads to a low correlation between endogenous variable and exdogenous variable.

A change in human behaviour depends upon people's interpretation of new information in terms of old information or past economic performances.

A change in policy regimes and discretionary macroeconomic policy implies an interaction between old information and new information.

We need to specify how expectations are formed.

We depart from the practice of assuming adaptive expectations and perfect foresight.

We assume that the speed at which individuals revise their expectations depends upon people's cognitive efficiency and the interaction between old information and new information.

This means that the speed of adjustment increases as the degree of relevance between old information and new information increases.

Our question is as follows.

What are the factors which determine the speed of adjustment?

Current macroeconomics literature has assumed that it is given and pre-determined.

Rational expectation models can be written as follows.

$$y_t = aE(y_{t+1}/t) + cx_t$$

Where $E(y_{t+1}/t)$ denotes the expectation of its value next period as well as on the variable x.

The above equation tells us that expectations are equal to the mathematical expectation of y_{t+1} based on information available at time t.

We assume that people know the model, the parameters a and c.

If we define $E(y_{t+1}/t)$ by $E(y_{t+1}/t) = E(y_{t+1}/I_t)$, the mathematical expectation of y_{t+1} based on the information set I_t, which includes $E(y_{t+1}/t)$ is equal to current and past values of other variables[1].

Although the information set is assumed to include current and lagged values of economic variables, the rational expectation model completely ignores an inferential process.

On the other hand, J.M. Keynes's economic model can be written as follows.

$$E(y_{t+1}/t) = c(h, e, i)$$

Where i denotes new evidence

e denotes a prior evidence

h denotes a hypothesis

c denotes a posterior confirmation

The interrelationship between i, e, h and c is as follows.

$$c = Lh$$
$$L = \beta i$$
$$\beta = \theta(i, e)$$

L, β = a parameter

θ = the degree of relevance

The above model tells us that changing economic variables are an increasing function of the degree of relevance between old information and new information.

Rational expectation theory completely ignores an inferential process.

On the other hand, J.M. Keynes's economic philosophy belongs to an inferential theory, according to this theory.

All economic policy makers have to do in order to achieve economic goals, is to give a private sector appropriate evidence of their intention to convey it.

Rational expectation theory assumes that expectations are equal to the mathematical expectation of y_{t+1} based on information available at time t.

This means that y depends upon the current expectation of its value next period.

The validity of this theory is conditional upon the fact that people know the model and have the perfect foresight.

The above argument tells us that economic fluctuations

emerge out of rational expectations.

However, J.M. Keynes has a different perspective.

This means that economic cycles are due to evolutionary transformations in human cognition.

He would argue that relevance has played an important role in them[2].

For example, economic bubbles or hyperinflation are due to an increasing tendency of the human cognitive system to maximize the relevance of the information it processes.

In other words, economic fluctuations are the result of allocating the available attentional resources to the processing of the most relevant available inputs.

This means that economic fluctuations such as hyperinflation, an overshooting of exchange rates, and economic bubbles are due to the fact that a degree of belief could be rational[3].

Economic fluctuations are due to the fact that people's knowledge or their hypothesis changes and therefore, their conclusions have new probabilities and new premises.

Relevance theory contributes to the explanation of how a degree of belief could be rational.

According to relevance theory developed by Deirdre Wilson and Dan Sperber, comprehension is a process of inherence based upon people's search for relevance.

This theory answers the reason why economic fluctuations occur.

Chapter 4 Cognition and J.M. Keynes's General theory

It also clarify the essence of J.M. Keynes's economic philosophy, a central theme of J.M. Keynes's General Theory can be explained as follows.

Economic policy makers must understand people's attention. attention tends automatically to go to what is most relevant at the time and therefore the effectiveness of macroeconomic policy depends upon the people's taking the policy to be relevant enough to be worthy of attention[4].

Note
(1) Oliver Jean Blanchard
Stanley Fischer
Lectures on macroeconomics
The MIT Press 1992 P257
(2) An input is relevant to an individual when it connects with available contextual assumptions to yield positive cognitive effects: for example, true contextual implications, or warranted strengthenings or revisions of existing assumptions.

Relevance theory claims that, because of the way our cognitive system has evolved, humans have an automatic tendency to maximise relevance.

As a result of constant selection pressure towards increasing efficiency, our perceptual mechanisms tend automatically to pick up potentially relevant stimuli, our memory mechanisms tend automatically to store and when appropriate retrieve potentially relevant pieces of knowledge, and our inferential mechanisms tend spontaneously to process these inputs in the most productive way.

This spontaneous tendency to maximise relevance makes it possible to predict to some extent which available stimuli people will pay attention to and how they will process them.
Deirdre Wilson and Dan Sperber
Meaning and Relevance

Cambridge University Press 2012 P279, 282

(3) To treat the logic of partial belief as the theory of the rationality of betting quotients may seem a far cry from Keynes's logical interpretation of probability.

But there is no doubt that Keynes's main motive in writing the Treatise was to explain how a degree of belief could be rational and thus not merely a matter of the believer's psychological make-up but one which all rational men under similar circumstances would share.

The collected writings of John Maynard Keynes
Volume VII
A treatise on probability Macmillan 1973 XXI

(4) Does the government have any way of avoiding hyperinflations?
One institutional provision is "backing" of the currency.

If the government provides a promise that one unit of currency can be exchanged at positive real value for goods (if goods are perishable, for a stream of goods), there cannot be hyperinflation.

The reason is that under hyperinflation the price of money would eventually be low enough that individuals would exchange their money against goods with the government.

From then on, the price of money could not decrease further.
Oliver Jean Blanchard
Stanley Fischer
Lectures on macroeconomics
The MIT Press 1992 P195

4.3 J.M. Keynes's economic philosophy and the trade cycle

J.M. Keynes's economic philosophy means that discretionary macroeconomic policy and a capitalist system based upon a laissez-faire leads to economic fluctuations.

Economic boom is caused by optimistic expectation, which leads to pessimistic expectation.

If discretionary macroeconomic policy leads to economic boom, then logic tells us that this policy leads to economic slump.

Misdirected investment is caused by government intervention, then the remedy for economic depression is a minimal intervention.

Expectations are unstable and therefore increasing investment is not a obvious economic solution for the recovery from depression.

If increasing consumption is an obvious solution, then the establishment of an ever normal granary is the only possible remedy.

The reason is that this system contributes to an increase in exchange of goods, which leads to an increase in consumption.

J.M. Keynes's economic philosophy means that expectations are destined to disappointment and economic boom is to end in a slump.

In other words, a higher rate of interest is not an obvious remedy.

According to J.M. Keynes, a small volume of investment and an increase in the propensity to consume by the redistribution of income is an appropriate remedy.

An increase in investment does not lead to employment and therefore expansionary monetary and fiscal policy do not mean J.M. Keynes's economic philosophy.

A minimal intervention is not destined to end in economic slump.

Economic boom includes economic slump, and economic slump includes economic boom[1].

This means that a laissez-faire capitalist system leads to overinvestment or uncontrolled and unplanned investment.

J.M. Keynes rejects expansionary monetary and fiscal policy or discretionary macroeconomic policy.

The acceptance is conditional upon the fact that this policy leads to an increase in consumption.

Note

(1) J.M. Keynes's economic philosophy means a minimal intervention because this intervention leads to the avoidance of economic fluctuations in a laissez-faire capitalist system.
J.M. Keynes says in the following way.

> In conditions of laissez-faire the avoidance of wide fluctuations in employment may, therefore, prove impossible without a far-reaching change in the psychology of investment markets such as there is no reason to expect.
> I conclude that the duty of ordering the current volume of investment cannot safety be left in private hands.
> When the disillusion comes, this expectation is replaced by a contrary "error of pessimism", with the result that the investments, which would in fact yield 2 per cent, in conditions of full employment, are expected to yield less than nothing and the resulting collapse of new investment then leads to a state of unemployment in which the investments, which would have yielded 2 per cent, in conditions of full employment, in fact

yield less than nothing.

We reach a condition where there is a shortage of houses, but where nevertheless no one can afford to live in the houses that there are.

Thus the remedy for the boom is not a higher rate of interest but a lower rate of interest.

For that may enable the so-called boom to last.

The right remedy for the trade cycle is not to be found in abolishing booms and thus keeping us permanently in a semi-slump, but in abolishing slumps and thus keeping us permanently in a quasi-boom.

John Maynard Keynes The General Theory of Employment Interest and money Macmillan 1949 p313-p332.

Chapter 5

J.M. Keynes's General theory and Yamada Houkoku's economic policy

5.1 An ever normal granary and Yamada Houkoku's economic policy

Yamada Houkoku was born on Feb 21 in Takahashi city of Okayama prefecture (Present) in 1805.

In 1860, he was appointed as finance minister of Bitchu Matuyama Han (a domain government). Yamada's successful career started in Bittyu Matuyama Han, where he made great contributions to education, military security, social welfare and economic development.

He worked out his philosophy of mercy for poor formers.

Faced with financial crisis economic depression and accumulated debts, he carried out revolutionary economic reforms.

He set up a government bureau for savings and investment, called "the Buikukyoku", and it was directed to investment in income-earning projects.

Bitchu Matuyama domain was rich in iron and coal.

The "Buikukyoku" lent money to his people and recommended them to make "Bitchu Guwa".

The making of them was conditional upon the fact that it promised to buy them back.

In other words, capitalist economy was based upon uncertainty and Bitchu Matuyama economy was based upon certainty.

In the capitalist economy with financial crisis and economic depression, an increase in money supply does not remove liquidity trap.

However, in the Bitchu Matuyama economy, an increase in money supply does remove liquidity trap.

"Bitchu Guwa" was sent to Edo and it contributed to the increase in agricultural products like rice in Edo.

In other words, "Buikukyoku" in the Bitchu Matuyama Han creates "creative creation" not destructive creation among Bitchu Matuyama's financial position, his people and the Edo economy.

In other words, Houkoku makes Bitchu Matuyama Han, his people and people in Edo happy at the same time.

Money supply from "Buikukyoku" creates effective demand, increase productivity between Bitchu Matuyama economy and Edo economy, and stabilizes product prices.

Money creation contributes to the reduction in Bitchu Matuyama's fiscal debts because "Buikukyoku creates huge profits for the Bitchu Matuyama's economy.

Yamada Houkoku's economic policy is based upon his philosophy of shimin buiku.

His economic policy includes the spirit and mind of mercy, sympathy love and caring for poor people.

The buikugata which means an ever normal granary is established by him.

This organization yields a huge profit which is used for the people in the Buichu Matuyama domain[1].

It is linked with the Buichu Matuyama Domain banknotes

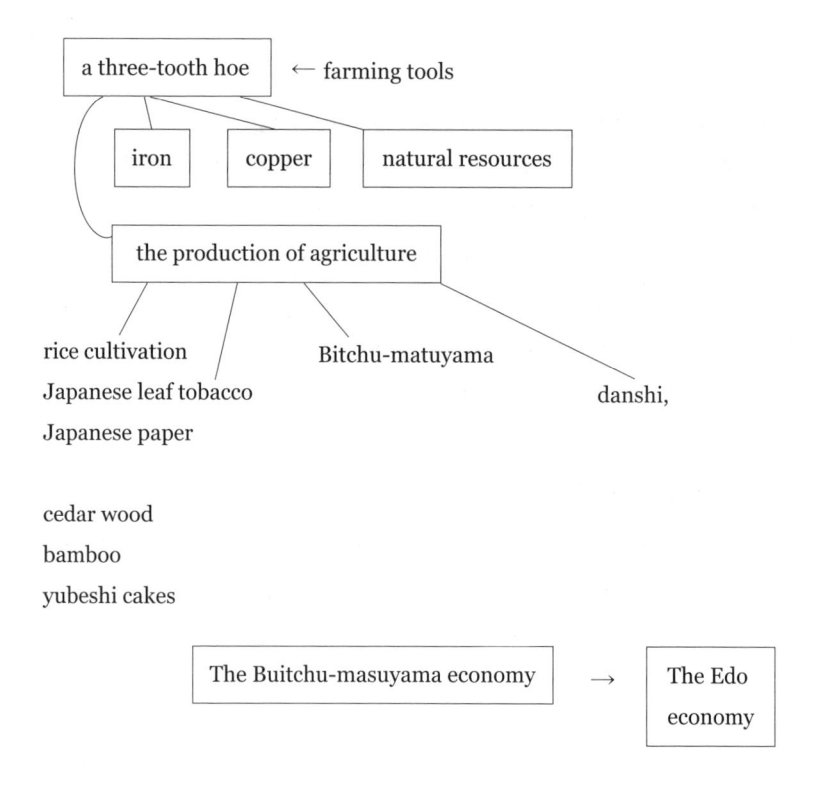

```
a three-tooth hoe   ← farming tools
    │
    ├── iron    copper    natural resources
    │
    └── the production of agriculture
           │
    ┌──────┼──────┐─────────────────┐
rice cultivation   Bitchu-matuyama
Japanese leaf tobacco              danshi,
Japanese paper
```

cedar wood
bamboo
yubeshi cakes

| The Buitchu-masuyama economy | → | The Edo economy |

Chapter 5 J.M. Keynes's General theory and Yamada Houkoku's economic policy

and has the right to lend and issue them.

Yamada Houkoku's financial rebuilding plan is based upon the establishment of an ever normal granary.

This organization called "buikugata" was created within the Bitchu-matuyama domain in 1852.

His financial reforms and economic policy is based upon the view that enriching the people enriches the country.

The following diagram explains the essence of his economic policy.

These products in the Buichyu Mastuyama domain contribute to an increase of output in the Edo

His economic policy implies an increase in exchange of economic goods, which is related with price fluctuations and the value of purchasing power in money.

An ever normal granary creates money and makes money creation which causes a multiplied effect on local and domestic economy.

The purpose of its establishment is to lend money and provide a financial assistance for poor people.

In other words, it will contribute to a reduction in unsold products and an increase in demand.

Its money creation is used for production purpose and therefore this does not lead to economic bubbles.

Yamada Houkoku created a purchasing power for people, allocating newly created money to the productive sectors.

It is not surprising that Yamada Houkoku was successful

in the economic reform.

The ever normal granary and economic growth were crucially linked.

People borrowed money from the ever normal granary and therefore additional purchasing power would be created.

Normally, the worry is that excessive money creation would result in a collapse in the value of paper money.

However, as long as the money is used for productive projects, and there won't be the collapse.

This means that there will be more output now if more money has been used for productive purpose.

In other words, more money has been created, but the money was used for investment and production so that the economy grew.

If both credit and output rise at the same time, then monetary value remains constant.

Yamada Houkoku's economic philosophy challenges conventional wisdom which means that money is neutral with respect to output [2].

His economic policy is inconsistent with new classical economics.

What Yamada Houkoku recognizes is that money creation increases the demand for new products.

An ever normal granary therefore simultaneously brings about both the demand for and supply of new products.

If Yamada Houkoku had created excessive money that was

Chapter 5 J.M. Keynes's General theory and Yamada Houkoku's economic policy

not used for investment purpose, prices would have been driven up.

The ever normal granary established by Yamada Houkoku contributed to the stability in prices.

In other words, the supply of money used in the economy was equal to that of products.

This means that the sum of the credit creation from the ever normal granary was used for necessary productive sectors.

A major reason for Yamada Houkoku's successful economic achievement was the establishment of the ever normal granary with the system of credit control.

In other words, that policy contributed to the reduction in fiscal debts, which "guided" credit to productive sectors.

The ever normal granary acted as the control center of the creation and allocation of purchasing power.

Thanks to the ever normal granary, called Buikukyoku, resources and money was allocated to industries of strategic importance, money was not used for unnecessary sectors or unproductive purposes.

Yamada Houkoku was in charge of providing the priority industries with funds.

He fully appreciates the importance of money for a growth-oriented economy.

His economic policy is based upon the creation and allocation of money.

He knows what money is.

This implies that money and barter is not separable.

In other words, money and an ever normal granary are related with each other.

Note

(1) Toru Nojima says in the following way.

While Houkoku Yamada was in charge of the domain government reforms, he steadfastly held on to shimin buiku, a concept which means creating a society in which life improves for everyone regardless of their social rank or how much money they make.

The Japanese word buiku means to show mercy on the people and teach them with love and caring.

Shimin buiku effectively laid the foundation of a movement in Japan called kokuri minpuku, which means creating profits for the land and improving the lives of people.

Industrial development, domain banknote reprinting, and other measures all helped to stabilize the lives and futures of the people who had previously been dealing with austerity and the policy also laid plans to create a wealthy domain and strong army.

Toru Nojima

Learning the key to successful reforms from Yamada Houkoku

Meitoku Publishing 2015 P94, 95

(2) Toru Nojima says in the following way.

To deal with its own financial difficulties, the Bitchu-matsuyama domain issued two types of banknotes.

The economic situation continued to deteriorate, however, and soon banknote exchange reserves bottomed out.

He knew how important it was to rebuild trust in the domain currency.

He understood that restoring faith in the currency and regaining the domain's credibility was the only way to free the people from their insecurity.

Chapter 5 J.M. Keynes's General theory and Yamada Houkoku's economic policy

In October 1852, Houkoku burned the gargantuan pile of banknotes in front of a large crowd.

Houkoku was well aware of the fact that if people lack complete access to their personal finances, the circulation of goods stops and the economy stagnates and collapses.

Later, Houkoku oversaw the large scale issuance of three new types of domain banknotes and used huge profits obtained from industrial development within the domain to build up the monetary reserves.

The new currency was called eisen and soon won the confidence of the people of the domain.

Toru Nojima
Learning the key to successful reforms from Houkoku Yamada
Meitoku Publishing 2015 P83, 89

If we apply Yamada Houkoku's solution to the resolution of a conflict between domestic objective and external objective, the following conclusion can be derived.

In order to resolve the conflict, the establishment of a global ever normal granary is needed for global prosperity.

The granary based upon international leadership and cooperation must create complementary economic network.

Faced with accumulated debts, external deficit and internal deficit, this organization which engages in the "buy and sell" transactions, contribute to an increase in the amount of exchange of goods.

External deficit in one country may lead to internal surplus in that country, thanks to the export to another country.

However external surplus in one country leads to external deficit in another country, which means internal deficit in the country.

In the long run the internal deficit in one country leads to internal deficit in another country.

However if an ever normal granary is successful in creating complementary economic network with complementary goods, then internal surplus and external surplus in one country leads to them in another country.

Yamada Houkoku does not view internal balance and external balance as separate.

If they are inseparable, the solution to the problem of international conflict between them is not worth studying.

Yamada Houkoku's economic policy based upon an ever normal granary implies the fact that savings and investment decisions are not made by different people.

The ever normal granary created by him makes it possible for them to make a cooperative activity.

J.M. Keynes's proposal for an international clearing union lacks the functioning of an ever normal granary.

Yamada Houkoku's economic solution can't be found in J.M. Keynes's General theory.

For Yamada Houkoku, the solution of a conflict between internal balance and external balance does not matter.

An increase in the amount of exchange of goods between countries is much more important than global liquidity.

J.M. Keynes tried to solve economic problems by the means of money, probably he believed that it plays an important role in economy.

On the other hand, Yamada Houkoku tried to solve them by the means of not only money but also human activities.

Human beings prefer exchange of goods to money as Adam Smith suggests.

We are inherently born with compassion and sympathy.

The economic system created by Yamada Houkoku is based upon complementary goods and complementary network.

This system implies that people supports each other.

Government does not control the market, but supports it.

Money, monetary policy and fiscal policy don't control it.

They just can support it.

There is a complementary relationship between money and goods.

There is also the same relationship between monetary policy and fiscal policy.

The establishment of an ever normal granary makes it possible for

Chapter 5 J.M. Keynes's General theory and Yamada Houkoku's economic policy

them to coordinate each other.

Money does not maximize the self-adjusting mechanism in a market economy.

On the other hand, no intervention in the market does not maximize it.

In other words, Yamada Houkoku's solution implies that the market economy in a capitalist economy lacks a self-adjusting mechanism and therefore, the establishment of an ever normal granary creates new capitalist economy which is inherently stable in terms of economic fluctuation or a trade cycle.

The ever normal granary created by Yamada Houkoku does not deprive economic transactions from a private sector.

The reason is that there is a complementary relationship between them.

J.M. Keynes's solution implies that Government intervention is separate from economic activity in a market.

Therefore discretionary macroeconomic policy may contribute to economic fluctuation.

In other words, there is a strong possibility that J.M. Keynes's solution involves risk and uncertainty.

This means that Government policy may create economic bubble, the collapse of it and therefore economic depression.

Human behaviour is uncertain and unpredictable.

People can't predict Government intervention and therefore there is a danger that an unpredictable policy causes an uncertain event.

In a complementary capitalist system, however, even a small shock never cause a chaotic fluctuation.

This means that we don't need Government intervention in this system.

The problem does not lie in macroeconomic policy.

Economic depression is purely a phenomenon which is derived from an unstable capitalist system.

If this is true, logic tells us that the solution for the recovery from economic depression is a stable capitalist system.

A flue dynamics literature says that a solitary wave is always stable even if it faces a big shock. Yamada Houkoku changes a chaos economy into a soliton one.

A chaos economy implies that even a small shock may lead to a devastating economic depression.

On the other hand, a soliton economy is the opposite of a chaos economy.

This economy implies that a small shock does not lead to economic depression and financial crisis.

A monetary economy does not maximize the amount of exchange of goods.

A barter economy with no money also doesn't do that.

A capitalist economy lacks a complementary market.

The economic system created by Yamada Houkoku maximises the amount of exchange of goods with a minimum detrimental effect of money on macroeconomy.

The Houkoku's solution implies that the establishment of an ever normal granary is necessary for an increase in the amount of exchange of goods.

Yamada Houkoku focuses attention upon how we should create a self-adjusting mechanism in the economy based upon an ever normal granary.

He creates economic system that people become rich as investment increases.

This system implies that an increase in investment is proportional to one in consumption, output and employment.

Supply creates its own demand thanks to the ever normal granary based upon complementary economic web.

A capitalist economy can't coordinate the spending plans of all the players in a market economy.

This disequilibrium can't be solved by macroeconomic policy.

Every market does not equate supply and demand in a capitalist economy.

This means that aggregate demand does not equal aggregate supply in the economy.

However, Yamada Houkoku's economic policy proves that this disequilibrium can be solved by the establishment of an ever normal granary.

Modern capitalist economy or a laissez-fair market economy does not have any mechanism to guarantee that supply equals demand.

Yamada Houkoku challenges the above argument, because he is successful in solving this disequilibrium.

What we should learn from economic policy of Yamada Houkoku is as follows.

His economic policy implies an increase in exchange of economic goods, which is related with price fluctuations and the value of purchasing power in money.

An ever normal granary creates money and makes money creation, which causes a multiplied effect on local and domestic economy.

The purpose of its establishment is to lend money and provide a financial assistance for poor people and a private firm, which suffers from a deficiency in demand and unsold products.

Its money creation does not lead to economic bubbles.

J.M. Keynes says in the following way.

As I now think, the volume of employment (and consequently of output and real income) is fixed by the entrepreneur under the motive of seeking to maximize his present and prospective profits.

It is true, that, when an individual saves, he increases his own wealth.

But the conclusion that he also increases aggregate wealth fails to allow for the possibility that an act of individual saving may react on someone else's wealth. John maynard Keynes The General Theory of Employment Interst and money macmillan 1949 P77-84.

If the above argument is true, J.M. Keynes's solution does not contribute to any reduction in the difference between them.

The reason is as follows.

Expansionary monetary and fiscal policy do not lead to an increase in the amount of exchange of goods and a division of labor.

An increase in both of them leads to both an individual's wealth and someone else's one.

The inconsistency in a capitalist economy can't be removed by discretionary macroeconomic policy.

In other words, The General theory does not say anything about the solution for this problem.

All of world economic problems may be due to the motive of seeking to maximize people's present and prospective profits.

On the other hand, Yamada Houkoku's economic policy makes it possible to achieve the objective that an individual behaviour increases someone else's wealth.

An ever normal granary creates money and control the amount of money.

Yamada Houkoku's solution means that an ever normal granary creates money for the purpose of increasing economic transactions, not financial speculation.

His policy implications are as follows.

The amount of money equals that of economic transactions.

The amount of money created multiplied by the velocity of money equals the amount of economic transactions.

If the above argument is true, the velocity of money is related with the number of division of labor and complementary economic goods.

He assumes that the amount of money created increases effective demand if supply of complementary economic goods creates its own demand.

Economic policy of Yamada Houkoku can be regard as the activity of Government enterprise or an ever normal granary which tries to reduce uncertainty.

If we are successful in transferring unexpected and uncalculated risk to Government enterprise, then the amount of economic transactions will increase.

Yamada Houkoku leaves the responsibility of risk and uncertainty to an ever normal granary.

An increase in economic transactions is related with the amount of exchange of goods and a division of labor.

The increase in both of them contributes to the stability in prices and purchasing power in money.

Yamada Houkoku's economic solution implies that money does not become an indispensable characteristic of an economy.

On the other hand, it implies that the amount of exchange of goods is an important characteristic of an economy in which economic activity does not depend upon expectation prone to variation.

J.M. Keynes's monetary theory of economics means that uncertainty plays a central role, while Yamada Houkoku's economic philosophy means that certainty plays a central role.

Yamada Houkoku's economic policy is based upon his philosophy of shimin buiku.

His economic policy includes the spirit and mind of mercy, sympathy love and caring for poor people.

The buikugata which means an ever normal granary is established by him.

This organization yields a huge profits which is used for the people in Buichu Matsuyama domain.

It is linked with the Buichu-Matsuyama domain banknotes and has the right to lend and issue them.

Yamada Houkoku's financial rebuilding plan is based upon the establishment of an ever normal granary.

The ever normal granary called "Buikugata" was created within the Bitchu-Matsuyama domain in 1852.

His financial reforms and economic policy is based upon the view that enriching the people enriches the country.

5.2 Economic network and Yamada Houkoku's solution

If we analyze Yamada Houkoku reform from the perspective of Richard Werner's economic theory, then the obvious reason can be found.

The reason why he succeeded is that Buikugata created a huge amount of money in the economy.

Houkoku makes a crucial decision of who will get money, which means "Hansatsu".

Richard Werners's theory can be explained in the following way. Providing money to key industries leads to an increase in purchasing power. As a result of this, domestic economy would be stimulated. Banks create new money and make a decision of who will get this money. And therefore their actions have a strong influence on consumption investment output and employment[1]. Yamada Houkoku makes new economic structure by creating and allocating money.

The ever normal granary established by Houkoku is engaged in a "buy and sell" economic transaction.

The establishment leads to the creation of money new economic structure and new demand.

They are mutually interdependent and therefore economic bubble and depression would not be found in the economic system.

If we follow his economic theory, economic disease such as economic slump inflation and deflation would never occur.

In a simplified way of saying, new classical economics implies no intervention in a capitalist market. On the other hand, J.M. Keynes's economics is related with Government intervention. A great difference between Yamada Houkoku's economic theory and modern macroeconomics is the recognition of the role of an interaction between them, which western economists haven't recognized the importance of it.

The Buikugate created by Yamada Houkoku can be recognized as an ever normal granary.

The organization includes and embraces the function of all economic activity.

The ever normal granary makes it possible for Yamada Houkoku to reduce uncertainty[2].

The reason is as follows. As the amount of information increases, the degree of uncertainty decreases.

Relevance theory explains the fact that people make a decision on the basis of both old information and new information.

This implies people's rational behavior.

An interaction between old information and new information creates economic fluctuation such as economic bubbles and financial crisis.

Yamada Houkoku is successful in achieving economic stability by creating "relevant" information.

In the Buitchu-Matsuyama economy, money creation industry structure demand and the amount of exchange of goods are mutually interdependent and "relevant" each other.

Yamada Houkoku seems to fully appreciate the role of money in economy.

He maximises the utility of money by creating an ever normal granary.

This means that money creates new industry structure new demand and an increase in the amount of exchange of goods, which leads to economic growth.

This will lead to an increase in output consumption investment and employment.

An interaction between money creation and the establishment of an ever normal granary must bring about economic boom.

We are obliged to admit that Yamada Houkoku knows what money is.

Money contributes to an increase in the amount of exchange of goods, which will bring about economic prosperity.

New classical economics denies the effectiveness of money creation.

Milton Friedman and J.M. Keynes recognize the role of money.

However, money creation and monetary expenditures alone do not necessarily mean an increase in the amount of exchange of goods.

In other words expansionary monetary or fiscal policy is not always effective with respect to output and employment.

On the other hand, Yamada Houkoku creates the environment in which the effectiveness of money is maximized. Therefore output investment consumption and employment increased in the Buichu-Matsuyama economy.

This implies that money creation and an ever normal

granary are linked together.

Evidence in the Buichu Mastuyama economy suggests the following argument.

If money creation and an ever normal granary are linked together output investment consumption and employment increase.

Note

(1) Richard Werner says in the following way

Providing money to key industries is only one side of the tasks authorities faced during the war effort, however.

As priority industries increasingly obtained purchasing power and laid claim to the available – and limited – national output prices would be driven up if consumption demand was not at the same time reduced.

The most important reason why war planners preferred bank funding as the main conduit of resource allocation was that banks create most of the money in the economy. And they make the crucial decision of who will get this money.

Their actions thus have a profound impact on equity growth efficiency and inflation.

By withholding purchasing power from one sector and allocating newly created money to another, the entire economic landscape can be reshaped.

Given this pivotal role of the banks, it is not surprising that the reform bureaucrats and war planners has developed a strong interest in them.

The German economists they read argued that banks and economic growth were crucially linked.

Economic growth can be accelerated if the inputs used – land labor capital and technology – are increased.

As we saw, the war bureaucrats had already found efficient ways of organizing the labor market and firms' management in order to ensure effective mobilization of land and human resources. The banks served as their main tool to maximize capital and technology inputs, direct resources and steer growth.

Richard Werner Princes of the yen Japan's Central Bankers and the transformation of the economy.

An East Gate Book 2003 P49, 50

By creating purchasing power for people, allocating newly created money to the productive sectors, it is not surprising that Yamada Houkoku was successful in the economic reform.

An ever normal granary and economic growth were crucially linked.

People borrows money from an ever normal granary and therefore additional purchasing power would be created.

Normally, the worry is that excessive money creation would result in a collapse in the value of paper money.

However, as long as the money is used for productive projects, that also increases output, and there won't be the collapse.

Although more money has been created, the money was used so cleverly that there is now also more output.

If both credit and output rise, then monetary value remains constant.

Yamada Houkoku's economic philosophy challenges the paradigm of new classical economics.

What Yamada Houkoku recognizes is that money creation increases the demand for new products.

An ever normal granary therefore simultaneously brings about both the demand for and supply of new products.

If Yamada Houkoku had created a huge amount of money that was not used for investment purpose, prices or would have been driven up.

(2) Mervyn King says in the following way

In a world of pure risk, where we can list possible future events and attach probabilities to them, there is a traditional view among economists of what constitutes rational behaviour - the so-called (optimising model, according to this view, individuals first evaluate each possible future outcome in terms of its impact on their well-being or (utility) and then weight each utility by the probability of the event to which it is attached, so deriving the average or 'expected utility' from a given set of actions, people are assumed to choose their actions (for example, how much to save today) in order to reach the highest level of 'expected utility', such optimising behaviour in a world of risk has proved a useful tool in analysing the impact of government interventions in markets and the provision of insurance against known risks.

In a world of radical uncertainty, where it is not possible to compute the 'expected utility' of an action, there is no such thing as optimising behaviour.

The fundamental point about radical uncertainty is that if we don't know what the future might hold, we don't know, and there is no point pretending otherwise.

Right through his life, John Maynard Keynes was convinced that radical uncertainty, as it has became known, was the driving force behind the behaviour of a capitalist economy as he explained, drawing on knight's distinction between the two types of uncertainty, there is an essential difference between a game of roulette or predicting the weather, on the one hand, and the prospect of war on the scope of new inventions, on the other.

Of the latter, he wrote about these matters. There is no scientific basis on which to form any calculable probability whatever. We simply do not know.

The language of optimisation is seductive, but humans do not optimise, they cope.

They respond and adapt to new surroundings, new stimuli and new challenges.

The concept of coping behaviour does not, however, mean that people are irrational. On the contrary, coping is an entirely rational response to the recognition that the world is uncertain.

There is no need to abandon the conventional assumption of economists that people prefer more consumption, or profit, to less, and that their choices display a degree of consistency.

The strength of economics as a social science is the belief that people will attempt to behave rationally. The challenge is to work out how a rational person might cope with radical uncertainty even smart people do not find it easy to know what it means to behave in a smart manner.

The main challenge to the economists' assumption of optimising behaviour, comes from 'behavioural economics', a relatively new field often associated with Daniel Kahneman, Richard Thaler and Amos Tversky.

Behavioural economics assumes that deviations from traditional optimising behaviour result from the fact that humans are hardwired to behave in a way that is 'irrational'.

The danger in the assumption of behavioural economics that people are intrinsically irrational is that it leads to the view that government should intervene to correct 'biases' in individual decisions or to 'nudge' them towards optimal outcomes.

But why do we feel able to classify behaviour as irrational?

Are policy makers more rational than the voters whose behaviour they wish to modify?

I prefer to assume that neither group is stupid but that both are struggling to cope with a challenging environment. After the crisis, the earlier belief that competitive markets were efficient and yielded rational valuation of assets was replaced by a conviction that financial markets were not merely inefficient but reflected irrational behaviour that produced 'bubbles' in asset prices and excessive demand for credit. Both views are extreme

(Marvyn King The end of alchemy money, banking and the future of the global Economy W. W. Norton & Company 2016 P129-133)

On the other hand, the view based upon schema attention and cognitive efficiency is very critical of them.

In other words, relevance theory and cognitive linguistics is in consistent with the theory of rational and irrational behaviour.

The reason can be explained as follows.

According to them, the degree of rationality and irrationality is purely a cognitive phenomenon.

Therefore, human assumption controls economic fluctuation in a capitalist market.

Unlike macroeconomic policy, Yamada Houkoku's economic policy means a change in human assumption. This implies an relevant interaction between seven policies.

5.3 Complementary economic network and Yamada Houkoku's solution

The emergence of new economic demand is conditional upon the fact that economic goods in one country and one in another country are complements each of the other.

Logic in a multiplied effect and chaos theory tells us that a private firm in one country creates new demand for another country.

The emergence of complementary economic web leads to an increase in division of labour exchange of goods and employment.

The creation of complementary Government enterprise leads to the emergence of complementary economic network.

One commodity in one region of one country is complementary to another commodity in another region of another country.

This means that each commodity has complementary character which the other commodity lacks.

Each commodity in world economy has complementary quality.

If this is true, then one of the causes of economic depression in the world is due to the fact that each commodity lacks the character which the other commodity holds.

Each commodity lacks the complete quantity needed or allowed to be purchased by consumers.

The emergence of economic bubble is negatively correlated with a great amount of effective demand home and abroad.

In other words, the collapse of economic bubble is positively correlated with lack of effective demand.

The solution for an increase in effective demand is the creation of complementary economic goods and the emergence of complementary economic web.

Yamada Houkoku's economic philosophy can be explained in the following diagram.

a multiplied increase in the amount of employment investment and consumption
an increase in new demand
The number of division of labour Complementary enterprise Complementary economic network Complementary economic goods

Yamada Houkoku's economic policy implies that there is a complementary relationship between monetary and fiscal policy.

J.M. Keynes completely ignores a complementary relationship between them.

He does not construct a theoretical model about its relationship between them.

The emergence of economic bubbles is positively correlated with the collapse of them.

On the other hand, the emergence of economic bubbles is negatively correlated with new demand for economic goods and investment, not expansionary monetary policy.

In other words, the emergence of economic bubbles is not positively correlated with expansionary monetary policy.

The reason is as follows.

If there is a great amount of effective demand in the economy, expansionary monetary policy leads to an increase in the amount of exchange of goods not one in the amount of financial assets such as currency, bonds, stocks.

If we analyze Yamada Houkoku's economic policy, the following conclusion can be derived.

Fiscal resources for public investment depend upon the profits from an ever normal granary, not government bond, taxes.

Monetary policy and fiscal policy seem to complement each other.

Fiscal revenues are intended for social welfare.

They do not depend upon government bond and taxes.

This supports the function of monetary policy effectively.

Fiscal policy means the establishment of an ever normal granary, which purchases and sells economic goods from a private firm.

Unlike J.M. Keynes, Yamada Houkoku's fiscal policy implies a reduction of uncertainty in an entreprenur's mind.

In J.M. Keynes's general theory both monetary policy and fiscal policy do not lead to an increase in certainty in an entrepreneur's mind.

A central characteristics of Yamada Houkoku's economic policy is complementarity.

In order to make both monetary and fiscal policy complement each other, the establishment of an ever normal granary is necessary.

The definition of "complementarity" means combining well to form a balanced whole.

For example, good beer is a complement to dinner.

One commodity goes well with another commodity.

For example, red wine makes an excellent complement to beef.

These two economic goods are complementary to each other.

If good beer is a complement to a good evening meal, then a similar logic can be explained in the following way.

The complementary relationship between monetary policy and fiscal policy is a complement to an increase in economic growth employment consumption and investment.

The following diagram explains a complementary economic network.

Chapter 5 J.M. Keynes's General theory and Yamada Houkoku's economic policy

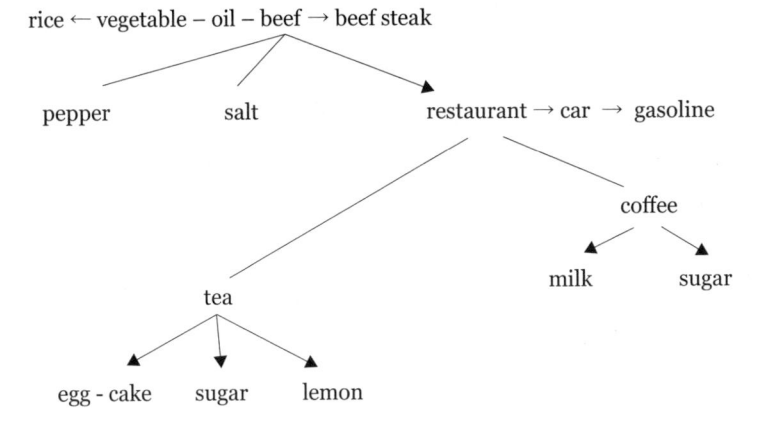

```
rice ← vegetable – oil – beef → beef steak

pepper        salt            restaurant → car → gasoline

                                              coffee

                                         milk      sugar
                      tea

         egg - cake   sugar   lemon
```

The above diagram explains the fact that supply creates its own demand.

This means that complementary goods and economic network of complementarity contribute to an increase in economic growth, employment and consumption.

Each commodity supports each other.

Different commodities create economic web of economic diversity.

In a global capitalist economy, expansionary monetary policy leads to the emergence of economic bubbles.

However, this policy leads to a real economic growth if a capitalist economy holds a complementary economic web of economic diversity.

Yamada Houkoku's economic policy challenges J.M. Keynes's argument that demand creates supply.

Supply can create its own demand, provided that an

additional commodity to the existing one creates emergence.

The supply of coffee does not always create its own demand.

On the other hand, the supply of coffee with milk creates new demand and an increase in consumption.

Yamada Houkoku's solution means that Government makes supply creates its own demand.

In other words, his economic policy means the establishment of an ever normal granary, which creates a complementary innovation.

As the result of this, the ever normal granary contributes to an increase in fiscal revenues.

On the other hand, J.M. Keynes's solution means that Government creates its own demand by its intervention in the market.

This implies that the intervention will lead to an increase in fiscal deficit.

Yamada Houkoku and J.M. Keynes are quite different in the point of the perspective of the role of Government.

According to Yamada Houkoku, an ever normal granary means Government enterprise, which supports a private firm.

On the other hand, J.M. Keynes regards Government as the organization which increases investment control taxes and changes interest rates.

J.M. Keynes completely ignores the role of Government, which maximises the amount of employment consumption and profit.

The ever normal granary established by Yamada Houkoku tries to maximize both its own profit and a private firm's profit.

In a global capitalist economy, a private firm tries to maximize its own profit.

However, she does not try to increase the amount of employment for the welfare of people and happiness.

Her own profit dominates social security in a society within a capitalist's mind.

Therefore, J.M. Keynes's solution or Government intervention such as monetary and fiscal policy contributes little to an increase in employment consumption and exchange of economic goods.

As long as the purpose of a private firm is the maximization of its own profit, J.M. Keynes's solution does not lead to an increase in employment and output.

Yamada Houkoku may fully appreciate the fact that investment uncertainty is negatively correlated with the degree of complementarity.

The definition of "complement" means the thing that goes well or suitably with something else.

In other words, complement things are ones which make it complete.

There is a complementary relationship between rice and a curry dish.

This means that rice makes an excellent complement to a curry dish.

J.M. Keynes's solution can't make a complementary relationship in world economy.

On the other hand, Yamada Houkoku succeeded in creating a complementary relationship between Government and enterprise.

Dillard Dudley says in the following way.

> When wealth-holders express a preference for hoarding money rather than lending or investing it, the production of real social wealth is handicapped.
>
> This preference for owning money rather than owning income-yielding wealth exists to a significant degree only in a world in which the economic future is uncertain.
>
> If the world were one in which the economic future could be predicted with mathematical certainty, there would be no sense in storing wealth in the barren money form.
>
> Only the highly uncertain nature of the economic future explains why there is a preference for storing wealth in the form of nonincome-yielding money[1].

Uncertainty is negatively correlated with the degree of complementarity.

In other words, the degree of certainty is proportional to an increase in complementarity in an economy.

Surface structure means economic phenomenon such as inflation unemployment and financial crisis.

On the other hand, deep structure controls surface structure.

The example of it is the things such as an uncertain capitalist system a policy regime economic structure human psychology, and human cognitive mechanism.

If the above argument is true, a change in deep structure is the solution for economic recovery.

The General theory does not provide us with any solution for a change in deep structure.

Yamada Houkoku's economic policy is quite different from expansionary monetary and fiscal policy (a traditional macroeconomic policy).

His solution is based upon the establishment of an ever normal granary which changes commodity prices.

Yamada Houkoku's economic mind implies that an increase in commodity prices leads to people's purchasing power in money.

Yamada Houkoku focuses attention upon how we should create a self-adjusting mechanism in the economy based upon an ever normal granary.

He created economic system that people become rich as investment increases.

This system implies that an increase in investment is proportional to one in consumption, output and employment.

A capitalist economy can't coordinate the spending plans of all the player's in a market economy.

This disequilibrium can't be solved by macroeconomic

policy.

Every market does not equate supply and demand in a capitalist economy.

This means that aggregate demand does not equal aggregate supply in the economy.

However, Yamada Houkoku's economic policy proves that this disequilibrium can be solved by the establishment of an ever normal granary.

Modern capitalist economy or a laissez-fair market economy does not have any mechanism to guarantee that supply equals demand.

Yamada Houkoku challenges the above argument, because he is successful in solving this disequilibrium.

What we should learn from economic policy of Yamada Houkoku is as follows.

A market economy which has a self-adjusting system creates economic situation that consumption in the future is coordinated among economic players.

A self-adjusting system, based upon an ever normal granary would remove uncertainty about price fluctuations and contribute to an increase in investment.

With the establishment of an ever normal granary, the coordination is possible.

This system makes it possible for household and business to coordinate their future spending plans in a capitalist economy.

The problem of coordination problem is not solved by the

General theory of J.M. Keynes.

An ever normal granary creates a fractal economic network and complementary economic goods.

This leads to an increase in a division of labour and the amount of employment.

An ever normal granary eliminates uncertainty from the market.

Any government intervention can't adjust the disequilibrium between supply and demand.

An ever normal granary changes economic structure into new structure, which eliminates uncertainty and economic bubbles.

Uncertainty implies people's money hoarding.

The granary makes it possible for the amount of money created to be equal to the amount of production.

As long as supply satisfys people's unrealized wants, the amount of supply is equal to that of demand.

An ever normal granary eliminates unsold products due to overproduction.

This means that new production lessens people's preference for hoarding money.

If one of the causes of economic depression is due to a disturbance in a self-adjusting market mechanism, the solution for economic prosperity is not monetary and fiscal policy.

The real solution must be the adjustment in a market structure.

An ever normal granary serves the function of a medium of exchange.

In other words, it functions as the organization for economic adjustment.

And therefore, money is not needed for economic transactions.

Richard Werner's economic theory tells us that money creation matters in a capitalist economy[2].

Yamada Houkoku provided money to people and key industries.

They obtained a purchasing power in money and therefore consumption investment and output increases.

Money creation caused by an ever normal granary contributed to their additional purchasing power.

The money was used only for productive projects, which led to an increase in output consumption and employment.

Also there would be a stable price in the economy.

That credit born out of an ever normal granary would create new demand.

It would simultaneously create both the demand for and supply of new goods.

A central characteristics of Yamada Houkoku's economic policy is as follows.

The creation of credit and complementary economic goods lead to the situation that Say's law hold valid.

Yamada Houkoku allocates credit to the key industries that bring about huge profits.

Chapter 5   J.M. Keynes's General theory and Yamada Houkoku's economic policy   99

As a result of this supply creates its own demand.

His economic policy can be explained by Richard Werner's economic theory.

Note
(1) Dudley Dillard
   The economics of John Mayhard Keyns
   Prentice-Hall, Inc 1948 P5-6
(2) Richard Werner
   Primces of the yen
      Japan's central Bankers and the transformation of the economy an East Grate Book 2003 P49-50

5.4 The Rizairon and Yamada Houoku's economic idea

The creation of government enterprise and discretionary macroeconomic policy belong to Government intervention.

However, they are different in character.

The former is not related with human expectation.

On the other hand, the latter depends upon it. In other words, the effectiveness of economic policy is determined by human expectation mechanism based upon cognition schema and background knowledge.

In case of market failure, it is no exaggeration to say that we need government intervention.

New classical economics is very critical of discretionary

macroeconomic policy, not economics of J.M. Keynes.

On the other hand, relevance theory supports the view that discretionary macroeconomic policy is effective.

However, this theory also supports the view that the policy is not effective with respect to output and employment.

It might be possible for the creation of government enterprise to change the existing old industrial structure into new emerging one.

The new structure will bring about the expansion of demand output and employment.

In case of economic bubble and financial crisis, the amount of money might not be equal to that of economic transaction.

If that is true, a decrease in demand output and employment is due to the fact that the amount of money does not match that of economic transaction.

The other side of logic tells us that the creation of new emerging market will lead to economic boom.

The emergence of economic bubble involves the collapse of it and financial speculation leads to the emergence of financial crisis.

If that is true, then the solution for economic prosperity is to relieve the cause of economic depression.

If one of the main causes of economic bubble or economic depression is due to the existing old industrial structure, then the answer is simple and easy for us to find.

If government is successful in changing that structure into

new emerging one, economic depression must change into economic boom.

In case of economic bubble and economic slump, the amount of money must be equal to that of economic transaction.

We also might say that money does not flow into every sector in domestic economy.

Therefore, consumption decreases and investment is reduced with the proportion to it.

Logic tells us that the amount of employment does not increase.

We could say that economic depression is purely due to the existing old industrial structure.

Any monetary or fiscal policy does not affect that structure.

If government investment monetary expenditures government enterprise and a private firm are successful in creating a new self-organizing "complementary" market, then domestic economy will come back to normal.

In our view, any economic fluctuation is purely the phenomenon which depends upon the existing economic DNA.

The solution Yamada Houkoku chose is the modification of the existing economic structure.

Yamada Houkoku's economic thought can be explained as follows. The deep structure controls the surface structure.

Economic phenomenon such as fiscal deficit and monetary stabilization belongs to the surface structure.

On the other hand, the current economic structure belongs

to the deep structure.

The creation of government enterprise creates new emerging market structure whose money flow into every sector in domestic economy.

Therefore, the emergence of economic bubble, financial crisis and economic depression could be avoided.

If Yamada Houkoku were alive now, he would say in the following way.

Economic depression will come back to normal if people try to help all the other people with sincerity and kindness.

The feeling mind and spirit of compassion and sympathy are inherent in human beings.

The book titled 「Learning the Key to successful reforms from Hokoku Yamada」 written by Toru Nojima explains the life and achievements of Yamada Houkoku[1].

His philosophy can be understood if we read The Rizairon which means Yamada Houkoku's fundamental economic ideas.

Economic boom or depression is strongly related with money.

Current macroeconomics in western countries depends upon the analysis of the function of money itself.

However Yamada Houkoku's economic theory is quite different.

The reason can be explained by the following diagram.

Chapter 5 J.M. Keynes's General theory and Yamada Houkoku's economic policy

money, profit, economic boom, fiscal debts
compassion, sympathy, justice, sincerity, moral feeling, vision

Money, profit, economic boom, a reduction in fiscal debts
An every normal granary, Coordination between people and exchange of goods
A welfare for all the people in the world
Compassion,

His theory is related with the relationship between money human mind and social policy concerned with education and industry.

Money goes to every people in every sector of the economy.

Compassion, sympathy and sincerity is strongly related with money.

Note
(1) The Rizairon Part I Generally speaking, the great rulers are those who can transcend problems nather than succumb to them, However, the people who are currently in charge of our finamces have all been swept away by this problem... Despite this, people continue to get tangled up in finamce issues, and only worry about trivial increases and decreases in the amount of money, These are the people who deal with finances, on the inside... Therefore, if we think about the great leaders and sages in history, all of them went beyond finances and stood on the outside. they refused to succumb to the problem and entrusted matters of the

treasury to officials they could trust, and they also stopped short of controlling this principle of government too rigidly, In addition, if we can follow their examples and stand outsind financial mattrs with our own ideas, bring morality to the fore and correct the hearts of people, improve public mosals, outlaw bribery and purge useless officials, work on improving civil government and enriching the people, place an importance on following the correct path and promoting education, and build up morale within the military and equip them with modern weaponry, then the politics will fall in line and the laws will be made clear. This great path of government must be initiated and the path of finance will surely follow suit.

Houkoku's Rizairon describes his view of how domain money and property should be used and could even be called a financial theory for the entire country. In part I of his economic treatise, Hokoku says that leaders who control matters in the world are those who can stand outside of things and not get swept away by them on the inside.

In other words, this key point in the Rizairon says that transcending financial problems can help people come up with ideas that view the entire situation and allow them to take holistic measures to deal with problems.

Toru Nojima

Learning the key to successbul reforms from Hokoku Yamada meitoku publishing 2015 P50-52

Supplements

Financial crisis Great Depression and New economics for global prosperity

People in the world now are not happy because of inequality of wealth in world economy.

This leads to a decrease in consumption, which causes economic depression.

It may lead to the emergence of economic bubbles, which is due to financial speculation.

The bubbles are inherently unstable and lead to the collapse, which tend to bring about the devastating depression and financial crisis.

An inequality of wealth leads to economic depression, because people are obliged to speculate in financial market.

This means that the production of economic goods does not lead to profits.

Therefore, they have an interest in financial investment, which leads to the emergence and collapse of economic bubbles.

If the real cause of economic depression is a lack of exchange of economic goods, then the solution is the establishment of an ever normal granary.

The reason is as follows.

This will contribute to an increase in the amount of exchange of goods, which contributes to the growth of economy.

In other words, the inequality of wealth will be reduced, and therefore consumption increases.

This means that an increase in it leads to the expansion of investment, which contribute to a decrease in unemployment.

Logic tells us that people don't take risks to make money and there is no room for economic bubbles to occur.

If Yamada Houkoku were alive now, he would propose the establishment of a global ever normal granary, which do "buy and sell" economic transactions.

This organization will not only provide finance but also contribute to the self-organizing emergence of a global economic web, which creates complementary goods.

The ever normal granary makes it possible for all the different participants to spend at the same time in domestic and international economy.

It may also make it possible for free capital mobility, flexible exchange rates and freedom of choice to be achieved at the same time.

Conventional wisdom in international macroeconomics literature says that it's impossible for the three regimes mentioned above to be achieved at the same time.

With the establishment of it, monetary policy can be intended only for the stability of exchange rates not domestic economy and investment.

Yamada Houkoku's solution implies that a country can

pursue to achieve both internal balance and external balance.

His solution is not consistent with Swan model.

If the ever normal granary is successful in an increase in the amount of exchange of goods and the creation of complementary economic goods, then both objectives can be achieved.

The reason is as follows.

External deficit leads to an increase in internal balance.

External surplus in domestic country leads to an increase in internal balance in foreign country.

Part II

Yamada Houkoku's solution for global economic prosperity "The transformation from a competitive global capitalism to a complementary economic system"

Introduction

An ever normal granary makes a monetary economy into an exchange economy.

J.B. Say's law means that supply creates its own demand.

Every producer who brings goods to market does so only in order to exchange them for other goods.

Whatever is produced represents the demand for another product.

Additional supply is additional demand.

The economy based upon an ever normal granary and money is more efficient than the one based upon only money.

Yamada Houkoku's solution means a creation of the situations in which Say's law holds.

The establishment of an ever normal granary implies that whatever is produced can be sold and misdirected production results in temporary oversupply.

The reason is as follows.

Oversupply of a private sector creates its own demand because of this establishment and its functions.

Excess production will be corrected by this organization.

This means that entrepreneurs leave responsibility to it which is in charge of a sales-promotion.

Yamada Houkoku's solution implies a denial of the

possibility of general overproduction and a deficiency of aggregate demand.

If we are successful in creating a capitalist economy based upon an ever normal granary and money. then there will always be a sufficient rate of spending to maintain full employment.

An ever normal granary issues money lends it purchases economic goods and creates economic network.

This means that the amount of money created is always equal to that of production whose stocks will be completely sold out.

1 A monetary economy and Yamada Houkoku's solution

According to new classical economics, a change in human behavior depends upon an unexpected noise.

In other words, the difference and gap between the actually realized results and the expected one determines economic fluctuation.

The above argument explains the central theme of J.M. Keynes's General Theory.

On the other hand, in order to develop this theory further, we need relevance theory developed by Dan Sperber and Deirdre Wilson.

J. M. Keynes's treatise on probability includes human cognition and the concept of relevance.

The General Theory is based upon it.

However this theory ignores the interpretation of new information and an inference process.

On the other hand, Yamada Houkoku seems to have understand them fully.

The equation of rational expectation hypothesis can be written as follows.

$$Y_t = EY_{t-1} + E_t$$

Where EY_{t-1} is the expected value formed previously of Y for the period t.

Y_t is the actual value of Y for period t and E_t is a random error term.

The hypothesis of it assumes that people make the best possible use of the limited information they have.

This means that the error term E_t is uncorrelated with any variable known at the time the expectation is formed and in particular any of its own lagged values[1].

On the other hand, if the error term E_t is relevant with any variable, the situations are much more complicated.

The point is how we should model the learning process.

According to a treatise on probability, by John Maynard Keynes, they make the forecast by the judgement of relevance.

He says in the following way.

> In the first we compare the likelihood of two conclusions on given evidence.
>
> In the second we consider what difference a change of evidence makes to the likelihood of a given conclusion.
>
> In symbolic language we may wish to compare x/h with y/h or x/h with $x/h_1 h$.
>
> We may call the first type judgements of preference or when there is equality between x/h and y/h of in difference and the second type.
>
> We may call judgements of relevance or when there is equality between x/h and $x/h_1 h$ of irrelevance.
>
> In the first we consider whether or not x is to be preferred

to y on evidence h.

In the second we consider whether the addition of h_1 to evidence h is relevant to x.

If h_1 and h_2 are independent and complementary parts of the evidence between them they make up h and neither can be inferred from the other.

If x is the conclusion, and h_1 and h_2 are independent and complementary parts of the evidence, then h_1 is relevant if the addition of it to h_2 affects the probability of $x^{(2)}$.

The above argument tells us in the following way.

J.M. Keynes assumes that actually realized results and expected ones are correlated.

If he were alive now, he would modify the equation of REH as follows.

$$Y_t = f(EY_{t-1}, E_t)$$

subject to the following equation

$$EY_t = f(Y_{t-1}, Y_{t-2}, Y_{t-3}, etc)$$

where EY_t is the function of an interaction between the previous variables.

$E_t > 0$ if EY_t and E_t are relevant, $E_t = 0$ if both of them are not relevant.

However the above model completely lacks human cognition and an inference.

Therefore relevance theory does work in making an theoretical model based upon J.M. Keynes's intuitive ideas.

Dan Sperber and Deirdre Wilson says in the following way.

> Some information is old, it is already present in the individual representation of the world.
>
> Unless it is needed for the performance of a particular cognitive task, and is easier to access from the environment than from memory, such information is not worth processing at all.
>
> Other information is not only new but entirely unconnected with anything in the individual's representation of the world.
>
> It can only be added to this representation as isolated bits and pieces, and this usually means too much processing cost for too little benefit.
>
> Still other information is new, but connected with old information.
>
> When these interconnected new and old items of information are used together as premises in an inference process, further new information can be derived: information which could not have been inferred without this combination of old and new premises.
>
> When the processing of new information gives rise to such a multiplication effect, we call it relevant.
>
> The greater the multiplication effect, the greater the relevance[3].

The above argument tells us that rational belief or expectation is the degree of relevance between old information and new information in human mind.

Relevance theory tells us in the following way.

Discretionary macroeconomic policy is not effective unless it affects people's expectation and their motives of seeking to maximize their present and prospective profits.

If we assume that the actually realized results are new information and the expected ones are old information then the new model may be derived, which is based upon J.M. Keynes's General Theory rational expectation and relevance theory.

The new classical theory is very successful in accounting for the correlations between revisions to output and unexpected increases in macroeconomic variables between them.

However, this theory can't explain the negative relationship.

On the other hand, J.M. Keynes's General Theory cannot account for the negative correlation between revisions to aggregate demand and discretionary macroeconomic policy.

Therefore we need the General theory of probability rational expectation and relevance theory.

If we are successful in making it, then this will contribute to the development of macroeconomics.

Our intuitive idea is as follows.

Expectation includes economic principle in human cognition cognitive efficiency people's search for relevance and the maximization of people's profits.

Economic fluctuation can be derived from the fact that

the factors mentioned above context and their encyclopedic knowledge interact each other.

A central theme of J.M. Keynes's General Theory can be explained as follows.

A difference between expected and realized results creates economic fluctuation a trade cycle and, the emergence and collapse of economic bubbles.

In other words, if there is little difference between them, then economy can be stabilized. Uncertainty in human mind will contribute to an increase in the difference between them.

According to J.M. Keynes's General Theory, a monetary economy is one in which changing views about the future can influence macroeconomic variables[4].

If they are correlated with uncertainty, then a reduction of it will lead to the stability of a capitalist economy.

What we should learn from Yamada Houkoku's economic policy is as follows.

A monetary economy with the establishment of an ever normal granary is successful in reducing it.

This means that a capitalist economy with a self-adjusting system is essentially one in which changing views about the future doesn't occur.

In other words, the system is not purely a monetary system in which uncertainty is able to affect the amount of output and employment.

Yamada Houkoku is successful in changing the Buitchu-Matsuyama economy into the system in which changing views about the future stimulates the economy.

The establishment of an ever normal granary contributes to a reduction in the accumulation of unsold stocks.

In a monetary economy, economic depression forces people to hold money.

The reason is as follows.

The amount of money which they choose to hold depends upon their incomes and the prices of the things.

However, with the establishment of it in a monetary one, the opposite occurs in a capitalist economy.

The slump doesn't oblige them to prefer liquidity, thanks to the fact that the amount of money holding is independent of them.

An ever normal granary can make the situation that the realized results are always equal to the expected ones.

The reason is as follows.

The establishment of an ever normal granary makes it possible for all economic players to consume invest and save any given sums simultaneously.

In other words, with this system, there is not any difference between the theory of economic behavior of the aggregate and the theory of the behavior of the individual unit[5].

The ever normal granary Yamada Houkoku creates (the Buikugata) implies a coordination between them.

In a monetary economy with an ever normal granary and a complex and complementary economic system, the interaction contributes to an increase in aggregate demand.

It may be possible for us to analyze the ever normal granary established by him from different perspectives.

The Buikugata created by Yamada Houkoku functions as the role of market places matchmaking and market design[6].

We could also regard it as the platform economy a homeostasis system and the system with a self-organization and complexity.

The concept of complementarity can be explained by the following argument.

Michael Portes says in the following way.

> Most industries are affected in some way by complementary products - that is, products that are used jointly with their product by the buyer.
>
> Computer software and computer hardware, for example, are complements.
>
> Complements are the opposite of substitutes, because the sale of one promotes the sale of another.
>
> Sometimes a number of complements are part of a firm's product line, while in other cases complements are supplied by other industries.
>
> Complementary products represent one type of interrelatedness among industries and raise important issues for a

firm's competitive scope[7].

If they emerge out of the interrelatedness, it may contribute to a reduction in uncertainty and fallacy of composition.

J.M. Keynes argues the importance of a willing and unimpeded exchange of goods and services in conditions of mutual advantage, which is not analyzed in detail[8].

However, they may represent the solution which he can't find in the General Theory.

Yamada Houkoku creates reaction networks by the establishments of an ever normal granary.

As a result of this, every people in the Buitchu-Matsuyama economy live happily.

His belief means that anyone of them don't suffer from poverty.

A destructive innovation leads to unemployment.

However, a creative innovation may lead to full employment.

He is very successful in energizing the reactions.

Government intervention based upon monetary or fiscal policy can't create the emergence of reaction networks.

On the other hand, no intervention in the market leads to the same result, which is supported by the argument of monetarism and new classical economics.

J.M. Keynes says that Government intervention is necessary in order to change an unstable market into a stable one.

He seems to believe that Government and the market are

in conflict.

In other words, his view implies that a capitalist economy can be divided by a Government sector and a private sector.

On the other hand, Yamada Houkoku creates a complementary relationship between Government and a market in the economy and this supports each other.

He tries to make use of everything including resources, goods and people in order to create new value.

The establishment of an ever normal granary is expected to bring happiness, sympathy, compassion and money to all the people in the Buitchu-Matsuyama economy.

Yamada Houkoku is successful in energizing a self-adjusting mechanism in the market by the function of it.

Note
(1) Patrick Minford
   Rational expectations macroeconomics an introductory hand book Blackwell 1992
(2) R. M. O'Donnell
   Keynes: philosophy, economics and politics macmillan 1989 P53-56
(3) Deirdre wilson and Dan sperber Meaning and Relevance Cambridge University Press 2012 P279-282
(4) John maynard Keynes
   The general theory of employment interest and money Macmillan 1949 P416
(5) John maynard Keynes
   The general theory of employment interest and money Macmillan 1949
(6) Alvin E. Roth

Who get what
William Collins 2016
(7) Michael E Porter
Competitive Advantage
Creating and sustaiming superior performance Free Press 2004 P416
(8) John maynard Keynes
The general theory of employment interest and money Macmillan 1949

2 Complex cognitive theory and Yamada Houkoku's policy

According to recent macroeconomic models, the objectives of economic policy can be achieved by a change in policy regimes with people who have rational expectation.

On the other hand, according to the deep structure model, they are achieved by the fact that policy makers provide evidence of their intentions and people inferring their intentions from the evidence.

Modern linguistics tells us that rational expectation model proves unsatisfactory because it fails to explain human creative aspect when people face a changing environment.

Macroeconomic policy implies new information.

A limited understanding of the real world is related with human search for relevance.

An imperfect understanding of the real world is due to human cognition based upon economic principle.

It tries to maximize utility with a minimum effect.

The gap between economic reality and human assumption is new information, which brings about economic fluctuations.

The interaction between three factors creates human misunderstanding in communication, economic recovery and the emergence and collapse of economic bubbles.

They include (1) human cognition which search for relevance

(2) human attention and (3) human background knowledge.

A change in policy regimes influences human assumption, which leads to economic fluctuation.

Economic philosophy of J.M. Keynes means the explanation of economic fluctuations based upon human cognition.

In a similar way, economic fluctuation is creates by them.

People's interpretation of an interaction between each policy might determine the emergence of new demand.

If the above argument is true, we could say that an interaction between "relevant" policies and systems creates a change in expectation.

Yamada Houkoku might create new theory of expectation based upon cognitive linguistics and complex science.

Cognitive linguistics is related with the concept of schema attention and relevance.

On the other hand, a central theme of complex science is an interaction between each variable.

Therefore the interpretation of an interaction between different policies influences people's expectation, which affects economic activity.

Yamada Houkoku is successful in creating the complementary economic network.

If each policy and system support each other, human cognitive mechanism works.

The reason is people's search for relevance.

This means that a change in policy regimes modifies people's expectation.

If people believe that they are relevant, a self-organizing economic network will emerge and create complementary goods.

Yamada Houkoku's solution might be related with the relationship between human cognition and a spontaneous emergence of economic network.

His economic policy stimulates people's search for relevance.

This means that a 'relevant' policy reduce uncertainty and risk in human mind.

This will lead to a spontaneous order of economic activities.

The creation of complementary goods and the search for relevance inherent in human mind are interdependent each other.

An interaction between them creates new demand.

The emergence of complementary economic network makes it possible to contribute to an increase in the J.M. Keynes's multiplier[1].

Therefore this leads to an increase in output consumption and employment.

Complementary economic network can be explained by the following example.

The iron might be made into forks, knives and spoons as well as axes.

The milk might be made into ice cream.

The wheat and milk might be made into a porridge.

Now at the next period, the French might consume what they had by way of renewable resources and the bounty of their first inventions or they might think about what else they could create.

Perhaps the ice cream and the grapes can be mixed or the ice cream and grapes mixed and placed in a baked shell made of wheat to create the first French pastry.

Perhaps the axe can be used as such to cut firewood.

Perhaps the wood and axe can be used to create bridges across streams.

You get the idea at each period the goods and services previously "invented" create novel opportunities to create still more goods and services[2].

The above argument implies a complex and self-organizing economy.

This means that the amount of product sold could be foreseen with certainty.

Therefore, economic depression would not occur.

The reason is a lack of the existence of uncertainty as to their profits in the future.

Yamada Houkoku's solution makes it possible for people to foresee the amount of product sold with certainty.

He is successful in removing liquidity preference from a monetary economy.

Note

(1) Furthermore, the schedule of marginal efficiencies will partly depend on the effect which the circumstances attendant on the increase in the quantity of money have on expectations of the future monetary prospects, and finally the multiplier will be influenced by the way in which the new income resulting from the increased effective demand is distributed between different classes of consumers.

Nor of course, is this list of possible interactions complete.

John Maynard Keynes
The General theory of employment interest and money
Prometheus Books
1997 P298-299

(2) Stuart Kauffman
At Home in the Universe
The search for the laws of self-organization and complexity
Oxford University Press
1995 P289, 290

3 Yamada Houkoku's solution and Generative Economics "Cognition and Universal macro-economics based upon modern linguistics"

Economic activity is the creation of new value and it can't be explained by the amount of money.

The following diagram explains the central theme of Yamada Houkoku's solution.

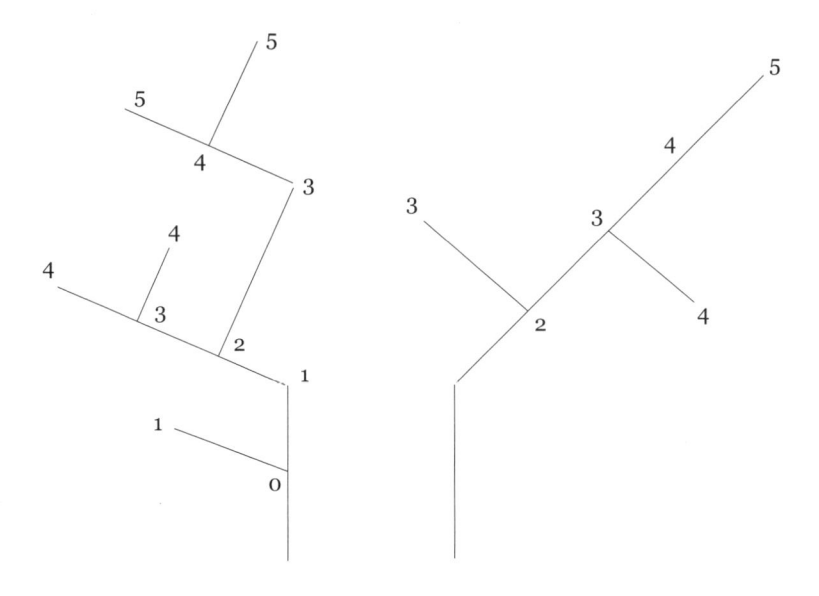

A fractal economic system means that pattern of the parts is exactly the same with that of the whole[1].

New value is based upon old value, then the amount of

exchange of goods output and employment increases.

One commodity is merged by another commodity on a fractal basis.

The degree of merger explains the amount of exchange of goods.

As the number of merger increases over time in the world economy. the disequilibrium in domestic objective and external objective in both countries will be reduced in the long run.

The above diagram is provided by J. Nelson[2].

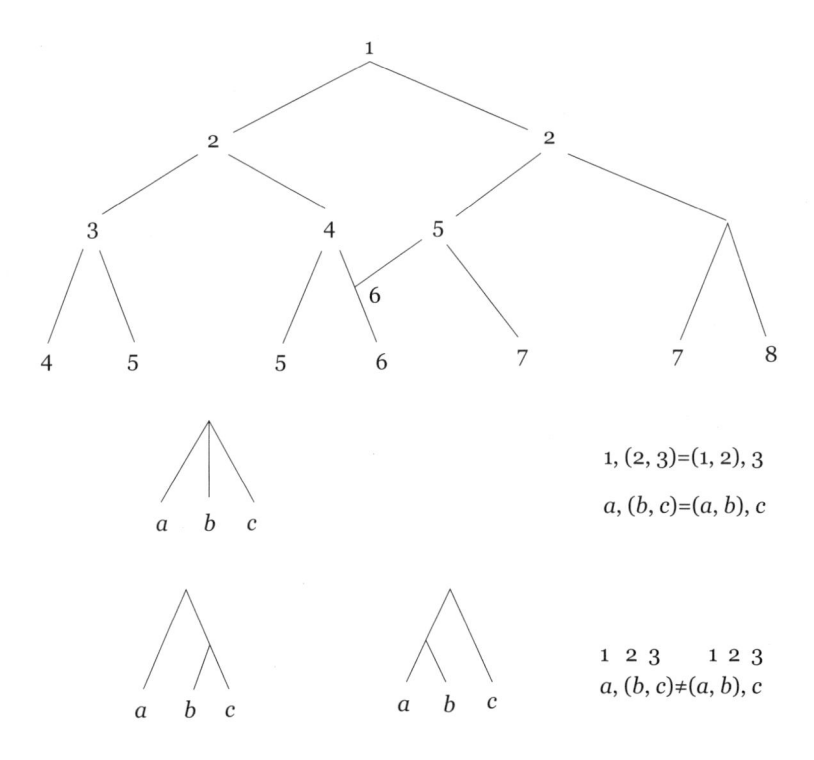

$1, (2, 3) = (1, 2), 3$

$a, (b, c) = (a, b), c$

$1\ 2\ 3 \quad 1\ 2\ 3$

$a, (b, c) \neq (a, b), c$

This means that different commodities on a fractal basis can be created.

By creating a fractal economic system in the world economy, the division of labor and the amount of exchange of goods will be increased.

This means that the amount of output and employment increases on a global basis.

Therefore, economic inequality will be reduced.

By increasing the degree of merge of different commodities in order to create new value in economic activity, economic depression can be avoided.

No intervention means that economic problem left unresolved.

Monetary expenditures never create new value in the economy.

In other words, monetary and fiscal policies don't contribute to the creation of it.

It must be emerged by the merge of different commodities.

A destructive innovation creates the emergence of unemployment, which results in the disequilibrium of domestic objective and external objective.

On the other hand, Yamada Houkoku's solution, which implies a creative innovation, creates the emergence of new employment, which leads to the equilibrium of them.

Yamada Houkoku transforms the Buitchu-Matsuyama economy into the one based upon a fractal system.

The degree of departure from a fractal system determines the possibility of economic depression.

The amount of employment output and consumption depends upon the number of economic network exchange of goods and division of labor.

J.M. Keynes proposes the international clearing union and the commod control system.

On the other hand, the economic system created by Yamada Houkoku includes the function of them an ever normal granary and a banking principle which makes a credit creation.

This system contributes to the emergence of complementary economic network.

Therefore, Yamada Houkoku's solution is better than J.M. Keynes's proposal.

J.M. Keynes pays special attention to the problem of restoring equilibrium to balance of payments in two countries.

Note
(1) "Syntactic computation in the human brain the Degree of merger as a key factor" by S. Ohta, N. Fukui & K. L. Sakai, PLOS ONE, Vol. 8, e56230, PP1-16, 2013
(2) "Syntactic computation in the human fraim the Degree of merger as a key factor" by S. Ohta, N. Fukui & K. L. Sakai, PLOS ONE, Vol. 8, e56230, PP1-16, 2013

4 Yamada Houkoku's dynamic economic system

This paper is a theoretical study into how Yamada Houkoku's credit policy interacts with aggregate economic activity.

The purpose is to prove that the positive feedback through asset prices and the associated multiplier effect are a major innovation in Yamada Houkoku's economic policy.

Yamada Houkoku's economic policy tells us in the following way.

Money is intended to replace a barter system of exchange in order to relieve people from bringing goods to market.

However, fiscal debts financial crisis and economic depression are due to the excess creation of money which exceeds the amount of exchange of goods.

What we should learn from Yamada Houkoku's reform and his solution for financial balance is as follows.

The solution for economic recovery is the creation of a barter system, which contributes to an increase in the amount of exchange of goods.

By increasing the amount of it, it will lead to a reduction in fiscal debts monetary stability and therefore economic recovery.

Even if people only supply goods with no money, economic transactions work smoothly with the establishment of an ever normal granary.

Unlike the Bretton Woods system, which lacked a banking principle, the Buikugata played an important role in money creation.

The Bretton Woods system lacks a banking principle and a self-adjusting mechanism.

The Buikugata is inherently stable in the sense that it is based upon a great amount of information and perfect insight.

The interaction between a banking principle and the function of an ever normal granary reduces "uncertainty" in human mind and fiscal debts.

Fiscal surplus and the stability in the value of currency emerge out of the self-organizing system.

As a chaos theory suggests, a small increase in the amount of exchange of goods leads to a multiplier effect in a domestic and international economy.

Even if people have no money to purchase goods, because of financial crisis, the establishment of an ever normal granary can contribute to the increase of it.

Unlike J.M. Keynes's general theory whose multiplier effect depends upon the marginal propensity to consume, Yamada Houkoku seems to assume that its effect is determined by the degree of complementarity and the number of economic network.

The "credit cycles" model by Kiyotaki and Moore explains the fact that the small shock to firm's net worth in period t causes them to increase their demand for goods in period t and subsequent periods[1].

Yamada Houkoku constructs the dynamic economic system which does not allow small shocks to generate large, persistent fluctuation in employment income and output.

This system means that the effects of shocks don't persist amplify and spill over to other economic sectors.

The reason is that the establishment of an ever normal granary allows the amount of exchange of goods to remain constant.

The Buikugata creates innovation and economic network for the product of complementary goods.

On the other hand, if the Bretton Woods system had purchased goods from other countries and sold them, it would have survived.

An intervention by an ever normal granary implies a small increase in the amount of exchange of goods.

This leads to an improvement of the financial position of a firm.

Therefore the demand for more labor increases.

The improvement of financial position in one sector affects that of other sector's positions.

The value of paper currency in the Bitchu Matsuyama economy is not solely determined by the expected future value of it.

It is also affected by the financial position and balance sheet position, including the value of its reserve currency.

Yamada Houkoku's economic solution can be analyzed as

follows.

He replaces silver based reserves with gold based reserves in order to increase the amount of paper currency in circulation.

In the Edo period in Japan, silver was depreciating in value in the Edo economy.

On the other hand, gold coins (reserves) were increasing in value in its economy.

The current value of reserves affects both the amount of financial assets and the degree of credit for paper currency.

Both of them also determine the amount of fiscal surplus (deficit).

The amount of financial assets due to speculation is positively correlated with the current value of reserves in the market.

The amount of investment in financial market increases as it increases.

The credit in paper currency is positively correlated with the amount of reserves.

The dynamic interaction between the amount of credit and the value of reserves turns out to be a powerful transmission mechanism by which economic depression financial crisis and fiscal debts are prevented to occur.

The dynamic interaction between the amount of credit the value of reserves and an ever normal granary turns out to be a powerful transmission mechanism by which the effects of shocks don't persist amplify and spread out.

Firm's debt/asset ratio is thus reduced.

The accompanying rise in paper currency and gold reserves improves the financial position of firms.

Yamada Houkoku is successful in increasing the amount of exchange of goods the value of reserves and the number of economic network, which is based upon complementary goods.

This will subsequently lead to an increase for more labor and investment.

A shock to net worth is recovered by the change in the values of firm's assets or liabilities.

The economic system Houkoku created does not allow the impact on asset prices and therefore net worth at the time of the shock to persist.

The effect of economic shock can be removed by the dynamic interaction between them.

The ideas in this paper can be traces back to "credit cycles", which describes the positive interactions between asset prices and collateralized borrowing[2].

In the Buitchu-Matsuyama economy, the gold reserves from the Edo economy in Japan produce profit.

Borrowers' credit limits don't exist, because the amount of the local paper increases in proportion to an increase in the amount of collateralized financial assets.

In other words, it produces profit, which contributes to an increase in the amount of exchange of goods.

The relationship between the goods in the Buitchu Matsuyama economy and the one in the Edo economy is complementary.

The relationship between them can't be explained by nonlinear limit cycles or the predator-prey model.

For example, imagine economic goods of the Buitchu-Matsuyama and Edo economy.

If the former rises, the latter that depends upon it also multiply.

On the other hand, as the latter grow in number, the former supports the latter.

Eventually, both of them grow.

This means that the number of the latter can start to increase with an increase in the number of the former.

That is, they don't oscillate, away from the steady state.

Both of them don't reach to the equilibrium path that converges back to the steady state.

The establishment of an ever normal granary stabilizes people's expectation for the future movement of economy.

Without the establishment of it, a liquidity trap would always occur.

In other words, it is inevitable and monetary policy is not effective with respect to output and employment.

The economic model in the Bitchu-matsuyama economy can be written down in the following.

$$(1)\ Y = \theta_1 \cdot A$$

$$(2)\ A = \theta_2 (C + I + G)$$

$$(3)\ C = \left(\frac{1}{1-R}\right) Y$$

(4) $R = \theta_3 E + \theta_4 N$
(5) $I = \theta_5 Ec + \theta_6 M$
(6) $M = \theta_7 P$
(7) $P = \theta_8 A$
(8) $G = \theta_9 T + \theta_{10} F$
(9) $T = \theta_{11} Y$

θ_i denotes coefficient for adjustment.

I denotes numbers.

Y denotes national income.

A denotes the amount of exchange of goods.

C denotes consumption.

I denotes investment.

G denotes government expenditures.

R denotes the multiplier effect, which depends upon the degree of complementarity among economic sectors within economic web.

Ec denotes expected consumption which means expectation about the future amount of consumption.

M denotes the degree of credit in currency.

P denotes the amount of reserves.

T denotes the amount of taxes.

F denotes the amount of financial assets.

The economic model Yamada Houkoku has in his mind can be explained as follows.

Uncertainty is strongly related with expectation about the

future amount of consumption.

Government expenditure is a function of national income.

Investment is the function of uncertainty about the future amount of consumption.

It is the function of the degree of credit in currency.

In other words, we assume that the former is negatively correlated with the latter.

We also assume that the amount of financial reserves for speculation increases as the value of paper currency rises.

An ever normal granary is linked with the amount of an increasing value in reserves.

Yamada Houkoku seems to assume that the other side of expectation is uncertainty and they are interdependent each other.

The Buikugata, which implies an ever normal granary, controls the amount of exchange of goods, which depends upon the number of economic network and complementary goods.

The amount of it depends upon the degree of complementarity among economic sectors within economic web.

Note
(1) Nobuhiro Kiyotaki and John moore
   Credit Cycles
      The journal of political economy, Vol.105, No.2 (Apr, 1997), PP211-248
(2) Nobuhiro Kiyotaki and John moore Credit Cycles
      The journal of political economy, vol.105, No.2 (Apr, 1997), PP211-248

5 Yamada Houkoku's solution and a self-adjusting mechanism

If Yamada Houkoku were alive now, he would transform the "competitive global capitalism" into a complementary economic system.

He would propose the following solution for global economic prosperity.

Government creates complementary economic network complementary economic goods and the number of complementary economic network.

Public expenditures and its investment are intended for the creation of complementary economic network in the economy.

This means that new demand in one region in one country creates new demand in the other of another country.

In other words, if every region in every country has a complementary relationship with each other, then a small difference in local region causes a big difference and a multiplied effect in world economy.

Modern macroeconomics ignores the following points

(1) The role of an ever normal granary

(2) The relationship between an increase in employment and an international division of labor

(3) How a willing and unimpeded exchange of goods and services will be achieved

(4) The relationship between an international division of labor and the amount of exchange of goods and services

A capitalist system is inherently unstable because imperfect knowledge leads to a calculation judgement or guess that demand is higher than it really is.

However, the Buitchu-Matsuyama economy is inherently stable because a self-adjusting mechanism works.

The reason is due to the establishment of an ever normal granary.

Yamada Houkoku assumes that a deficit creates a surplus.

On the other hand, western economists assume that a surplus means a reduction in a deficit.

This implies that a reduction in absorption leads to a surplus in an external balance.

However, economic policy of Yamada Houkoku tells us that an increase in domestic demand creates a balance of payment surplus.

If he were alive now, he would say in the following way.

There is not a conflict between a deficit and a surplus.

If he were alive now, he would say in the following way.

This is not a conflict between a deficit and a surplus.

An increase in domestic demand may lead to a reduction in a balance of payment deficit.

In other words, an increase in absorption leads to a deficit in an external balance unless we succeed in creating complementary economic network.

Trevor Swan and James Meade ignore the time element and a complementary relationship.

A deficit in balance of payment in the short run may lead to the surplus in the long run.

In a similar way, an increase in absorption in the short run may lead to the surplus in the long run, although the deficit in balance of payment occurs in the short run.

The ever normal granary purchases goods from private firms and sells it to them.

This organization increases consumption and investment.

It also creates a fractal economic system, which leads to an increase in the amount of exchange of goods.

We assume that there is a complementary relationship between internal balance and external balance.

If the relationship between internal balance and external balance in one country is complementary, an conflict between them can be solved by the establishment of an ever normal granary.

In a similar way, a conflict between fiscal debt and demand management can be solved by it.

J.M. Keynes seems to assume that Government and private sectors are divided.

He also assumes that internal balance and external balance are separate.

Therefore he tried to solve the conflict between them.

However the application of J.M. Keynes's General theory

to international issues is not successful in bringing a mutual benefit to everyone in the world.

On the other hand, Yamada Houkoku's solution based upon the ever normal granary implies the creation of economic diversity.

Its creation transforms the competitive economy into the harmony one which makes complementary innovation.

This will stimulate domestic demand.

We try to apply Yamada Houkoku's economic policy to the solution of international issues now.

The answer can be written down in the following way.

A lack of complementary economic network, a hegemonic stability and a coordination failure may result in world economic crisis.

The accumulated fiscal debts can not be reduced only by macroeconomic policy.

The reason is simple. Monetary and fiscal policy don't always contribute to an increase in the amount of exchange of goods.

Western economists such as J.M. Keynes, Trevor Swan and James Meade assume that a conflict between internal objective and external objective must be solved at the same time.

However, we can't divide them and remove the interaction between them.

Yamada Houkoku creates complex economic network which

leads to an increase in the amount of exchange of goods.

His solution is intended for the welfare of poor people who want to improve their standard of living.

The system contributed to an increase in output consumption and income.

Unlike western economists, Yamada Houkoku assumes that a deficit and a surplus can't be divided.

In other words, he considers that internal balance includes external balance.

This means that absorption and current account balance interact each other.

Therefore, current account deficit may contribute to an increase in absorption (domestic demand).

The above argument tells us that current account deficit may result in an increase in national income.

The same logic can be applied to the analysis of the fact that a deficit in external balance in the short run may lead to the surplus in the long run.

Western economists completely believe that domestic and external objectives can be achieved by exchange rate and macroeconomic policy.

However, if there is the complementary relationship between them, economic policy based upon dynamic optimization is not effective in solving the conflict.

Macroeconomic policy based upon optimal control theory is not effective.

The reason is rational expectation and the interaction between Government and private sector.

In a similar way, J.M. Keynes's solution is not effective because of the interaction between domestic demand and current account balance.

If they are stationary, he may be right.

However they are non-stationary and therefore we can't achieve both of them at the same time.

The historical lesson from Yamada Houkoku's economic policy tells us in the following way.

The only solution is economic transformation based upon the concept of complexity and complementarity.

J.M. Keynes completely ignores the theory of complexity.

On the other hand, Yamada Houkoku's solution includes the creation of economic network, a fractal economic system, rational expectation, the theory of complexity and a centrally planned economy.

A laissez-fair economy means a lack of a change of policy regimes.

If it is related with the creation of economic network, human cognitive mechanism contributes to a well-functioning of macroeconomy.

The emergence of new economic network is impossible to occur without any intervention in the market.

However, it does not always work in a capitalist economy.

Unless each policy regime is relevant and interdependent,

human cognitive mechanism doesn't work.

In other words its relevance affects human expectation, economic activity and the effectiveness of a change in policy regime.

J.M. Keynes says that expectation determines the amount of economic activity[1].

However, human cognitive mechanism dominates and controls the movement of expectation.

J.M. Keynes's solution means that discretionary macro-economic policy controls human expectation.

On the other hand, Yamada Houkoku's ideas are as follows.

If one network is linked with another network by the establishment of an ever normal granary, it contributes to the emergence of a self-organizing economic network.

Therefore the amount of employment consumption and investment increases.

New economic network emerges out of the interaction between each network, which determines the amount of economic transactions.

Yamada Houkoku's assumption is as follows.

The import from other countries contributes to an imcrease in the demand in domestic economy.

Evidence suggests that the export of the Buitchu-Matsuyama economy to the Edo economy doesn't reduce the demand in its economy.

This means that the import to domestic economy doesn't lead to a decrease of absorption in another country.

Therefore Swan and Meade models are not adequate for explaining the working of the Buitchu-Matsuyama economy.

This implies that there is not a conflict between domestic objective and external objectives.

The following diagram explains the essence of Yamada Houkoku's ideas.

Yamada Houkoku's model

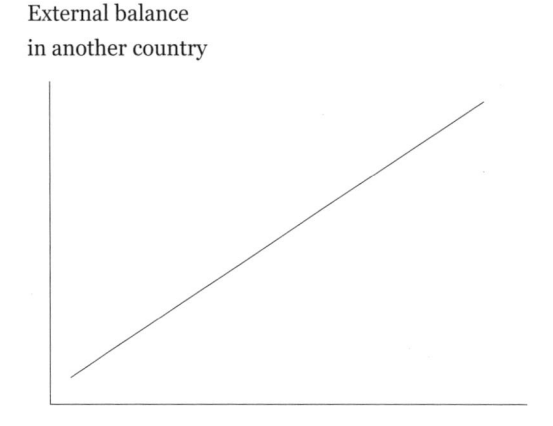

External balance
in another country

Absorption
(domestic demand)
in one country

external balance
in one country

absorption
in one country

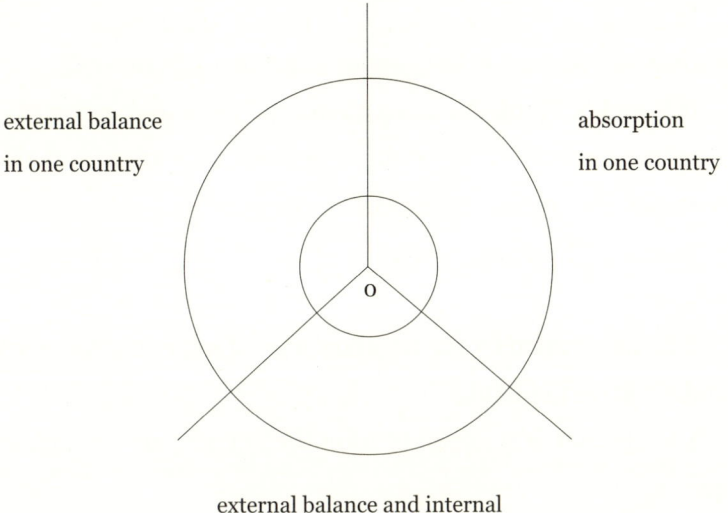

o

external balance and internal
balance in another country

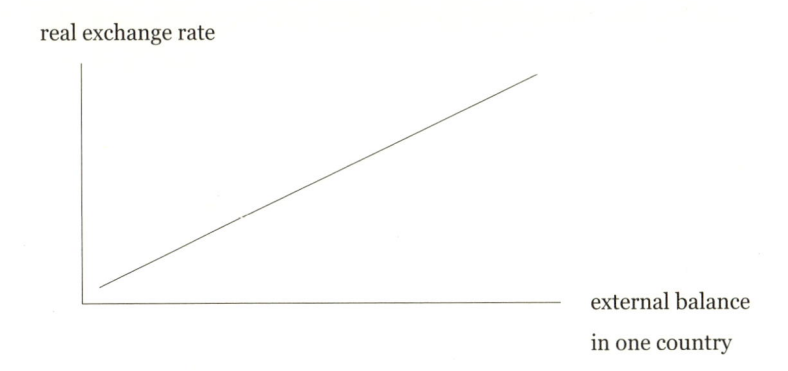

real exchange rate

external balance
in one country

    Yamada Houkoku's solution means new theory of expectation that each policy and system support each other.

    This implies that human cognitive mechanism works if they are relevant.

In other words, a change in policy regimes modifies people's behaviors. if they understand that it is rational.

If Yamada Houkoku were alive now he would argue that a "complementary" economic system is better than the "competitive" global capitalism.

Yamada Houkoku seems to assume that the amount of employment depends upon the number of division of labor.

It is determined by the number of complementary network and effective demand.

The amount of it depends upon the amount of exchange of goods.

Therefore Yamada Houkoku's solution can be written down as follows.

Government should create complementary economic network complementary economic goods and the number of complementary economic network.

Public expenditures and investment must be intended for the creation of complementary economic network.

Economic diversity leads to an increase in the amount of effective demand.

It makes supply create its own demand.

Complementary economic web makes comparative advantage work in international economy.

It also creates complementary economic goods and services which reduce uncertainty for the future in human mind.

Modern macroeconomics ignores the following points.

The first is the role of an ever normal granary.

The second is the relationship between an increase in employment and an international division of labor.

The third is how a willing and unimpeded exchange of goods and services will be achieved.

The fourth is the relationship between an international division of labor and the amount of exchange of goods and services.

Yamada Houkoku's solution seems to answer the above questions.

A complementary economic system makes the fact that international trade leads to a willing and unimpeded exchange of goods and services in conditions of mutual advantage.

It will contribute to an increase in the amount of exchange of goods at a local and global level.

We have the hypothesis that a change in the degree of merge between each variable or each commodity changes economic structure.

If this is true, Yamada Houkoku's solution can't be found in J.M. Keynes's economics.

His ideas mean that by changing it, a complementary economic structure and innovation will be created.

The Keynes's model can be written down in the following way.

$$Y = C + I + G + (X - M)$$

Y = national income

C = consumption

I = investment
G = Government expenditures
X = export
M = import

On the other hand, the Houkoku model is as follows.
$$Y = f(c, I, G, X, M)$$
$$C = \theta_1(I, G, X, M, Y)$$
$$I = \theta_2(c, G, X, M, Y)$$
$$G = \theta_3(c, I, X, M, Y)$$
$$X = \theta_4(c, I, G, M, Y)$$
$$M = \theta_5(c, I, G, X, Y)$$

θ_1 can be determined by the degree of relevance complementarity and merge between economic goods.

i denotes numbers.

Yamada Houkoku's solution tells us that what Government should do is to increase its degree of them.

Evidence supports the above argument.

In the nineteenth century, Britain had a huge current account surplus, although she suffered from a trade deficit.

This means that both countries were happy with economic activities.

Britain created complementary economic network between her and developing countries.

A multilateral payment system means the number of

economic network.

The British balance of payment in the nineteenth century was generally favorable and therefore large credit balances were earned.

It allowed her to invest large sums abroad, which contributed to economic development in other countries[2].

Evidence suggests that there is a high correlation between fiscal deficit and financial crisis[3].

If Government continues to increase fiscal expenditures in order to balance domestic disequilibrium, accumulated fiscal debts lead to currency crisis.

If Yamada Houkoku were alive now, he wouldn't increase fiscal expenditures.

In order to increase domestic demand, he would establish the commod control system, which J.M. Keynes proposed.

This system is concerned with an increase in the amount of exchange of goods.

It also deals with a profit-taking between selling and buying of commodities.

Therefore, Government takes a huge profit, which leads to fiscal surplus.

This means that the establishment of an ever normal granary contributes to the prevention of financial crisis and the collapse of economic bubble.

The creation of complementary goods is necessary in order to increase international competitiveness in one country and an increase of domestic demand in another country.

This means that a country in a balance of payment deficit recovers from economic depression.

In other words, exchange rate devaluation is unnecessary.

In order to balance it, we assume that an international policy coordination is extremely difficult as the literature upon international macroeconomics suggests.

If we apply Yamada Houkoku's ideas to the solution of a conflict between internal balance and external balance, the following conclusion could be derived.

Public investment must be intended for an increase in the amount of exchange of goods.

A central theme of the Swan diagram means that internal and external balance must be considered at the same time.

However Yamada Houkoku's solution implies that they should not be separated.

In other words, it seems to emphasize that there is not a conflict between both of them.

If we consider the relationship between internal and external balance in terms of the amount of exchange of goods, the different conclusion must be derived.

An increase in domestic production does not always worsen a position in the balance of payment.

Therefore the attempt to achieve internal balance and external balance doesn't need to be considered together.

J.M. Keynes divides macroeconomy into Government sector

and private sector.

On the other hand, Yamada Houkoku doesn't divide it into them.

In a modern capitalist economy any economic activity doesn't work without the holding of money.

However, without it, Yamada Houkoku makes it possible for people to engage in economic transactions.

The reason is as follows.

The former implies that the role of money and the activity of the exchange of goods are not divided.

The latter means that they support each other.

In other words, there is a complementary relationship between them.

If that is true, any small economic shock does not lead to a destructive economic depression.

Conventional wisdom in international macroeconomics literature says that a reduction in asset prices leads to economic slump.

However, Yamada Houkoku's solution proves that economy will come back to normal without fiscal expenditures.

The establishment of an ever normal granary reduces "uncertainty" in human mind.

In other words it contributes to increase "probability" in it.

This means that the degree of confirmation and confidence is maximized by the addition of new information.

Any mathematical equation doesn't explain human decisions and people's intuition.

J.M. Keynes considers that there is a conflict between domestic objective and external objective.

On the other hand, Yamada Houkoku seems to think that external objective and domestic objective supports each other.

This means that a balance payment deficit contributes to an increase in domestic demand, which brings about economic growth.

If we are successful in creating economic system that a balance payment surplus in one country leads to an increase in domestic demand in foreign country. international policy coordination is not necessary.

In a similar way, if a balance payment deficit in one country leads to an increase in absorption, discretionary macroeconomic policy and a competitive exchange rate depreciation is not necessary.

The solution for creating the above situations can be found in economic policy of Yamada Houkoku.

Historical lesson tells us that the establishment of an ever normal granary contributes to a complementary economic system.

This means that both domestic objective and external one are a complement each other.

The creation of international stabilization fund is necessary, which is intended for making complementary economic goods.

The international monetary fund must be based upon the function of an ever normal granary.

We must create economic system whose economic intervention is not necessary.

That system is not supposed to be affected by even a small shock.

Global capitalist system now lacks the function of an ever normal granary and complementary economic network.

J.M. Keynes proposes the solution that demand management can bring about an increase in output and employment.

He also makes a proposal that international clearing union provides one country the market for export in foreign country.

His solution means the demand management based upon the export of one country to foreign country.

On the other hand, Yamada Houkoku's ideas implies complementary economic network between the import from foreign country and demand in domestic economy.

By creating economic web mentioned above, the domestic economy in both one country and foreign country grows together.

J.M. Keynes emphasizes the importance of international liquidity.

On the other hand, Yamada Houkoku pays attention to the amount of exchange of goods.

An increase in monetary expenditures does not always

contribute to economic growth.

The expansion in domestic economy depends upon the amount of economic transaction.

Therefore, the establishment of an ever normal granary is indispensable for economic stability.

Domestic economy may suffer from a balance payment deficit in the short run.

However, if this leads to an increase in output and employment, then time allows the demand to increase.

Therefore the export to foreign country becomes higher.

This means that the domestic objective and the external one in both one country and foreign country are in equilibrium in the long run.

It is a logical conclusion that both of them don't suffer from unemployment balance payment deficit and economic slump.

World economic slump can be avoided by complementary economic web.

If financial crisis is due to economic depression and the disequilibrium in both of them, then logic tells us that the solution is the establishment of an ever normal granary.

As long as the granary and the commod control system are engaged in increasing the amount of exchange of goods and complementary economic goods, world economic crisis never occur.

Therefore, global capitalist economy doesn't need to be reformed.

One of the great mistakes J.M. Keynes made is as follows.

Supply does not create its own demand and discretionary macroeconomic policy is effective with respect to output and employment.

However, supply creates its own demand, provided that it is related with complementary goods.

Discretionary macroeconomic policy does not always stabilize people's expectation.

Probability is related with people's degree of uncertainty in their mind.

This policy does not always increase and control their degree of certainty.

The economic system Yamada Houkoku created does not need stabilization policy.

The reason is that it holds an ever normal granary, which means a self-adjusting mechanism.

Yamada Houkoku fully appreciates the importance of an ever normal granary.

With a market which has a self-adjusting mechanism, supply always equal demand in the future.

J.M. Keynes did not focus attention upon how we should create a self-adjusting mechanism in a laizze-faire market.

The problem is not a laizze-faire market.

The real problem is the fact that the market does not hold a self-adjusting mechanism.

Yamada Houkoku focuses attention upon how we should

create a self-adjusting mechanism in the economy based upon an ever normal granary.

He created economic system that people become rich as investment increases.

This system implies that an increase in investment is proportional to one in consumption output and employment.

An ever normal granary makes supply create its own demand, thanks to complex economic web.

A capitalist economy can't coordinate the spending plans of all the players in a market economy.

This disequilibrium can't be solved by macroeconomic policy.

Every market does not equate supply and demand in a capitalist economy.

This means that aggregate demand does not equal aggregate supply in the economy.

However, Yamada Houkoku's economic policy proves that this disequilibrium can be solved by the establishment of an ever normal granary.

Modern capitalist economy or a laissez-faire market economy does not have any mechanism to guarantee that supply equals demand.

Yamada Houkoku challenges the above argument, because he is successful in solving this disequilibrium.

What we should learn from economic policy of Yamada Houkoku is as follows.

A market economy which has a self-adjusting system create economic situation that consumption in the future is coordinated among economic players.

The self-adjusting system based upon an ever normal granary would remove uncertainty about price fluctuations and contribute to an increase in investment.

With the establishment of an ever normal granary, the coordination is possible.

This system makes it possible for household and business to coordinate their future spending plans in a capitalist economy.

The existence of coordination problem is not solved by the General Theory of J.M. Keynes.

Yamada Houkoku's economic policy and J.M. Keynes's General Theory is very similar, because both of them have a great interest in an ever normal granary.

However, it is no exaggeration to say that the solution of Yamada Houkoku is better than J.M. Keynes's economics.

An ever normal granary makes a monetary economy into an exchange economy.

It creates a fractal economic network and complementary economic goods, which leads to an increase in division of labor.

This brings about an increase in the amount of employment.

Under this system, supply creates its own demand.

If Government intends to establish an ever normal granary, the argument of classical economics holds valid.

An ever normal granary eliminates uncertainty from the market.

Without any government intervention, Government can adjust disequilibrium between supply and demand.

An ever normal granary changes economic structure into new structure, which eliminates uncertainty and economic bubbles.

Uncertainty implies people's money hoarding.

This system makes it possible for policy makers to create economic situations that macroeconomic policy does not lead to economic depression.

The reason is as follows.

The amount of money created is equal to the amount of production, because of the establishment of an ever normal granary.

Expansionary monetary and fiscal policy based upon it can create a complex economic system.

This system is a self-organizing economic structure whose supply creates its own demand.

The supply means complementary economic goods which creates new demand.

As long as supply satisfies people's unrealized wants, the amount of supply is equal to that of demand.

An ever normal granary eliminates unsold products due to overproduction.

This means that new production lessens people's preference

for hoarding money.

If one of the causes of economic depression is due to a disturbance in a self-adjusting market mechanism, economic solution is not monetary and fiscal policy (money creation).

The real solution must be the adjustment in a market structure.

An ever normal granary serves the function of a medium of exchange.

And therefore, money is not needed for economic transactions, an ever normal granary functions as the organization for economic adjustment.

Yamada Houkoku insures people's safe life against economic fluctuation which is inherent in risk and uncertainty.

Expansionary monetary and fiscal policy can't insure a stable purchasing power in money for people against them.

Discretionary macroeconomic policy might increase risk and uncertainty human mind as new classical economics suggests.

If risk and uncertainty in a capitalist economy leads to people's irrational decisions, logic tells us that a reduction in them is the solution for economic prosperity.

The capitalist economy based upon an ever normal granary allows policy makers to make discretionary macroeconomic policy for acceptance of full employment.

Under the system, there can be no general overproduction as long as supply creates its own demand.

If errors result in excess production of some particular items of output, it will be corrected when entrepreneurs shift from the production of things they cannot sell (at a profit) to the production of things they can sell (at a profit).

Say's law implies that the possibility of general overproduction never occur, which leads to the possibility of a deficiency of aggregate demand.

An ever normal granary makes it possible for all the different participants to spend at the same time in domestic and international economy.

Yamada Houkoku's economic policy is quite different from expansionary macroeconomic policy.

Houkoku's solution is based upon an ever normal granary whose function is to change commodity prices.

This solution leads to an increase in people's purchasing power in money.

Houkoku's economic mind implies that an increase in commodity prices leads to an expansion in output and consumption.

Yamada Houkoku's solution can be explained in the following way.
(1) Supply creates its own demand
(2) With the establishment of an ever normal granary and complementary economic market, economic activity does not depend upon expectation uncertainty and probability

(3) In other words, the essential properties of money would be lost and therefore economic activity must be stimulated
(4) The above argument implies that supply creates its own demand
(5) Expectations are prone to variation as the new classical economic with rational expectation suggests
(6) Yamada Houkoku's economic solution implies that money does not become an indispensable characteristic of an economy.
(7) On the other hand, it implies that the amount of exchange of goods is an important characteristic of an economy in which economic activity does not depend upon expectation prone to variation
(8) J.M. Keynes's monetary theory of economics means that uncertainty plays a central role

On the other hand, Yamada Houkoku's economic philosophy means that certainty plays a central role.

We assume that Yamada Houkoku regards an ever normal granary as an homeostasis in a human body[4].

Note
(1) John maynard keynes
   The general theorg of employment interest and money Macmillan 1949
(2) Peter Temin and David Vines
   The leaderless economy

Why the world economic system fell apart and how to fix it
Princeton University press 2013 P21-24
(3) Carmen M. Reinhart
Kenneth S. Rogoff
This time is different Eight centuries of financial Folly
Princeton University Press 2009
(4) Walter Brafford Cannon
Wisdom of the body
Kegan paul, Trubner and company 1932

6 Yamada Houkoku's solution for global economic prosperity

What we should learn from Yamada Houkoku's economic policy is as follows.

The establishment of an ever normal granary prevents a small shock from occurring large, persistent fluctuations in output and asset prices.

This means that the establishment of it engaged in economic transactions not only provide finance but also contribute to the emergence of a self-organizing economic web and complementary goods.

Yamada Houkoku's solution can't be found in J.M. Keynes's economics.

J.M. Keynes seems to ignore the fact that an increase in the amount of exchange of goods between countries is much more important than global liquidity.

He tried to solve economic problems by the means of money.

Probably he believed that it plays an important role in economy.

On the other hand, Yamada Houkoku tried to solve them by the means of not only money but also human activities.

Human beings prefer exchange of goods to money as Adam Smith suggests.

If we follow Adam Smith's wealth of Nations, the following

conclusion can be derived.

The division of labor depends upon a propensity in human nature to exchange.

The amount of it is determined by the extent of the market, which means the power of exchange.

An increase in the amount of exchange of goods leads to the emergence of money.

It is due to the inconveniency of a barter economy.

The certainty of being able to exchange determines the amount of consumption.

Adam Smith says in the following way.

> The wealth of a neighboring nation, however, through dangerous in war and politics, is certainly advantageous in trade.
>
> In a state of hostility it may enable our enemies to maintain fleets and armies superior to our own, but in a state of peace and commerce it must likewise enable them to exchange with us to a greater value and to afford a better market, either for the immediate produce of our own industry, or for whatever is purchased with that produce.
>
> As a rich man is likely to be a better customer to the industrious people in his neighborhood, than a poor, so is like a rich nation.
>
> A rich man, indeed, who is himself a manufacturer is a very dangerous neighbor to all those who deal in the same way.

All the rest of the neighborhood, however, by far the greatest number, profit by the good market which his expense affords them.

A nation that would enrich itself by foreign trade is certainly most likely to do so when its neighbors are all rich, industrious and commercial nations[1].

The above argument tells us that the amount of exchange of goods depends upon the richness of both parties.

This means that it is determined by the complementarity in a capitalist economy.

We are inherently born with compassion and sympathy.

The economic system created by Yamada Houkoku is based upon complementary goods and economic network.

This system implies that people supports each other.

Government does not control the market but supports it.

Yamada Houkoku is successful in making the linkages between the diversity of economic sectors in economic growth.

J.M. Keynes's model is based upon aggregate demand aggregate supply money growth interest rate and other aggregated factors.

John Maynard Keynes seems to ignore models of connections between various economic sectors.

The ever normal granary is intended for the creation of economic web, not the control and intervention in the market.

If different economic sectors support each other, then new demand will be created.

The definition of effective demand in Adam Smith and J.M. Keynes is quite different.

On the other hand, Yamada Houkoku seems to define it as new demand based upon a spontaneous order which can be derived from the laws of economic complementarity and substitutability.

If we regard the establishment of an ever normal granary as a change in policy regimes, then macroeconomic policy must be effective with respect to output and employment.

The reason is as follows.

The coordination among economic agents is instantaneously achieved.

Supply and consumption will be balanced and a value in money and prices will be stabilized.

The amount of employment will be increased by an increase in the amount of division of labor.

An increase in effective demand will contribute to it.

Yamada Houkoku's economic philosophy can be explained in the following way.

(1) Fiscal surplus

(2) No government intervention

    No control of complementary economic web

(3) Supply creates its own demand

(4) The creation of complementary goods

(5) The establishment of an ever normal granary restricts money to only the function of exchange of goods
(6) A common characteristics between J.M. Keynes's General Theory and Yamada Houkoku's economic policy is an ever normal granary.
However, J.M. Keynes does not make a theoretical framework based upon an ever normal granary
(7) Follow the movement of a market economy
(8) The emergence of new demand by creating complementary goods
(9) Fiscal revenues can be derived from Government enterprise's profits and speculation in goods and money
(10) Government enterprize creates new demand for private firm.
It creates new demand for Government enterprise
(11) The creation of a complementary relationship between Government enterprize and private firm is necessary for economic recovery
(12) If private firm in one country creates demand for one in another country, then global competition and inequality never occur, which may lead to global depressed economy
(13) Global economy implies that the world is interdependent.
Therefore chaos theory works
(14) World depressed economy is due to the fact that one

country in world economy does not support each other
(15) Economic depression in the world economy is not purely a monetary phenomenon
(16) In other words, economic depression is due to a lack of the number of a complementary economic web
(17) A lack of it leads to a reduction in the amount of exchange of goods
(18) It leads to a deficiency in effective demand
(19) Its deficiency leads to unemployment deflation and economic depression
(20) Yamada Houkoku's solution is not expansionary monetary and fiscal policy for stabilizing expectation
(21) His solution means the creation of complementary economic network.

The establishment of an ever normal granary must contribute to the emergence of complementary economic goods
(22) J.M. Keynes proposed the establishment of World Bank and International Monetary Fund
(23) Unlike J.M. Keynes, Yamada Houkoku's solution means that the creation of complementary economic network in one region of one country leads to new demand in another region of another country
(24) This implies that economic depression in world economy changes into the recovery, provided that every government try to construct complementary economic

web

(25) The emergence of new economic demand is conditional upon the fact that economic goods in one country and one in another country are complements each of the other

(26) Logic in a multiplied effect and chaos theory tells us that a private firm in one country creates new demand for another country

(27) The emergence of complementary economic web leads to an increase in division of labor, exchange of goods and employment

(28) The creation of complementary economic network leads to the emergence of complementary Government enterprize

(29) One commodity in one region of one country is complementary to another commodity in another region of another country.

This means that each commodity has complementary character which the other commodity lacks.

Each commodity in world economy has complementary quality

(30) If this is true, then one of the causes of economic depression in the world is due to the fact that each commodity lacks the character which the other commodity holds

(31) Each commodity lacks the complete quantity needed

or allowed to be purchased by consumers

(32) The emergence of economic bubble is negatively correlated with a great amount of effective demand home and abroad.

In other words, the collapse of economic bubble is positively correlated with lack of effective demand

(33) The solution for economy to come to normal is the creation of complementary economic goods and the emergence of complementary economic web

Note
(1) Adam Smith
　The wealth of Nations
　A Bantam Book
　2003 P622-623

Conclusion

Yamada Houkoku's economic ideas cannot be understand without some knowledge of modern linguistics and complex science.

People's interpretation of an interaction between each policy determines the emergence of new demand and a spontaneous system.

If the above argument is true, we could say that an interaction between "relevant" policies and systems creates a change in expectation.

Yamada Houkoku might create new theory of expectation, which is based upon both cognitive linguistics and complex science.

Cognitive linguistics is related with schema attention and relevance.

In the other hand, complex science is an interaction between each variable.

Therefore an interaction between different policies influences people's interpretation of it.

Yamada Houkoku is successful in creating a complex and complementary economic network.

If each policy and system supports each other, human cognitive mechanism works.

The reason is people's search for relevance.

This means that a change in policy regimes modifies people's expectation.

If people believe that they are relevant, a self-organizing economic network will emerge.

And it will also create new demand and complementary economic goods.

Yamada Houkoku's solution might be related with the relationship between human cognition and a spontaneous emergence of economic network.

His economic policy stimulates people's search for relevance.

A "relevant" policy will reduce uncertainty and risk in human mind.

J.M. Keynes says in the following way.

> Furthermore, the schedule of marginal efficiencies will partly depend on the effect which the circumstances attendant on the increase in the quantity of money have on expectations of the future monetary prospects.
>
> And finally the multiplier will be influenced by the way in which the new income resulting from the increased effective demand is distributed between different classes of consumers.
>
> Nor, of course, is this list of possible interactions complete [1].

This may imply that the multiplier is influenced by the

number of complementary goods.

Yamada Houkoku might assume that the investment multiplier depends upon a complementary economic network.

If this is true, the emergence and collapse of economic bubbles does not occur in a capitalist economy based upon money.

Without this network, monetary expenditures will go to financial assets.

This means that the "Austrian School" of economics explains the real movement of economy well.

Murray N, Rothbard says in the following way.

> Mises' business cycle theory was being adopted precisely as a cogent explanation of the Great Depression, a depression which mises anticipated in the late 1920s. But just as it was being spread through England and the United States, the Keynesian revolution swept the economic world, converting even those who knew better[2]

However, in the Buitchu Matsuyama economy based upon a monetary economy, misesian cycle theory doesn't hold valid.

Note
(1) J. M. Keynes
    The General Theory of Employment Interest and money

Macmillan 1949 pp298-299
(2) Ludwig von mises
The theory of money and credit
Yale University Press 1953 p16

References

Adam Smith
  The Wealth of Nations
  Bantam Classics 2003 p622-623
Alvin E. Roth
  Who gets what-and why?
  William Collins 2016
Carmen M. Reinhart
Deirdre Wilson and Dan Sperber
  Meaning and Relevance
  Cambridge University Press 2012
Deirdre Wilson and Dan Sperber
  chapter 27 Relevance theory
  The Handbook of Pragmatics edited by Laurence L. Horn and Gregory Ward
  Blackwell Publishing 2004
Dudley Dillard
  The Economics of John Maynard Keynes
  The Theory of a Monetary Economy
  Prentice Hall, Inc. 1948
George Lakoff
  Women, Fire and Dangerous things
  What categories reveal about the mind
  The University of Chicago Press 1987
John Maynard Keynes
  The General theory of employment
  Interest and money
  Prometheus Books 1997
John Maynard Keynes
  The General Theory of Employment, Interest, and Money
  Macmillan 1949
Kenneth S. Rogoff

This time is different
Eight centuries of financial Folly
Princeton University Press 2009
K.M. O'Donnell
Keynes : Philosophy, economics and politics
Macmillan 1989
Ludwig von Mises
The theory of money and Credit
Yale University Press 1953
Marvyn King
The End of Alchemy
Banking and the Future of the Global Economy
W. W. Norton & Company 2016
Michael E, Porter
Competitive Advantage
Creating and sustaining superior performance
Free Press 2004
Noam Chomsky
Rules and Representations
Basil Blackwell 1982
Noam Chomsky
Aspects of the theory of syntax
The MIT Press 1965
Noam Chomsky
A language
Chomsky's classic works
Language and in one volume
Responsibility and reflections on language
The New Press 1998
Noam, Chomsky
Verbal Behavior, by B. F. Skinner Reviewed by N. Chomsky
Language, vol.35, No.1, pp26-58, 1959
Nobuhiro Kiyotaki and John Moore
Credit Cycles

The journal of political economy, vol. 105, No.2 (Apr, 1997), pp211-248
Oliber Jean Blanchard and Stanley Fischer
  Lectures on Macroeconomics
  The MIT Press 1992
Patrick Minford
  Rational Expectations Macroeconomics
  An Introductory Handbook
  Blackwell 1992
Peter Temin and David Vines
  The leaderless economy
  Why the world economic system fell apart and how to fix it
  Princeton University Press 2013
Paul Davidson
  The Keynes solution
  The path to global economic prosperity
  Macmillan 2009
Richard Werner
  Princes of the yen
  Japan's central Bankers and the transformation of the economy
  An East Gate Book 2003
Robert P. Morphy
  The politically Incorrect Guide to the Great Depression and the new Deal
  Regnery 2009
Rudolf Carnap
  Logical Foundations of Probability
  The University of Chicago Press 1950
Stuart Kauffman
  At home in the Universe
  The search for the laws of self-organization and complexity
  Oxford University Press 1995
S.Ohta, N. Fukui & K. L. Sakai
  Syntactic computation in the human brain
  The Degree of merger as a Key factor
  PLOS ONE, vol.8, e56230, pp1-16, 2013

Thomas J. Sargent
Rational expectations and inflation
Hyper Collins College Division 1986
Toru Nojima
Learning the key to successful reforms from Yamada Houkoku
Meitoku Publishing 2015
Walter Bradford Cannon
Wisdom of the body
Kegan Paul, Trubner and Company 1932

■ **Auther**

Yasuhisa Miyake

  Yasuhisa Miyake lived in the apartment where J. M. Keynes had lived in London, while studied economics at University of London. He was born on February 21 when Yamada Houkoku was born.
  He is currently a founding general-secretary of Yamada Houkoku Research Association and teaches economic policy of Yamada Houkoku at Okayama University. He is also the author of "Cognition, Macroeconomics and Economic Policy of Yamada Houkoku", (University Education Press, 2012) and an ever-normal granary and J. M. Keynes's economic philosophy (University Education Press 2017)
  502 Koyama, Okayama City, Okayama Prefecture Japan 701-1352
  E-mail:koukoku0221m.jp@gmail.com

An ever normal granary and the solution for globaleconomic prosperity
—— What we should learn from J. M. Keynes and Yamada Houkoku ——

2019 年 12 月 28 日　初版第 1 刷発行

- ■ 著　　者 ──── 三宅康久
- ■ 発 行 者 ──── 佐藤　守
- ■ 発 行 所 ──── 株式会社 **大学教育出版**
  〒700-0953　岡山市南区西市 855-4
  電話（086）244-1268　FAX（086）246-0294
- ■ 印刷製本 ──── モリモト印刷㈱

©Yasuhisa Miyake 2019, Printed in Japan
検印省略　　落丁・乱丁本はお取り替えいたします。
本書のコピー・スキャン・デジタル化等の無断複製は著作権法上での例外を除き禁じられています。本書を代行業者等の第三者に依頼してスキャンやデジタル化することは、たとえ個人や家庭内での利用でも著作権法違反です。

ISBN978-4-86692-061-0